MANAGING OFF-SITE STAFF FOR SMALL BUSINESS

Lin Grensing-Pophal, SPHR

Self-Counsel Press
(a division of)
International Self-Counsel Press Ltd.
USA   Canada

Self-Counsel Press acknowledges the financial support of the Government of Canada through the Book Publishing Industry Development Program (BPIDP) for our publishing activities.

Printed in Canada.

First edition: 2001, Second edition: 2010

Library and Archives Canada Cataloguing in Publication

Grensing-Pophal, Lin, 1959-

      Managing off-site staff / Lin Grensing-Pophal. — 2nd ed.

Previous edition published under title : Telecommuting.

ISBN 978-1-55180-865-9

      1. Telecommuting. 2. Small business — Management. I. Title.
HD2336.3.G73 2009   658.3'12   C2009-902766-6

The "Telecommuting Safety Checklist" on page 40 and the "Telecommuting Agreement" on pages 159–162 are reprinted with permission of the US Office of Personnel Management. "Managing Telecommuters: Tips for Supervisors" on page 131 is reprinted with permission of the University of Texas — Houston Health Science Center. "Teleworking Issues" on page 130 and the "Telecommuting Policy" on page 147 are reprinted with permission of AG Communication Systems. The self-assessment on page 65 and "Common Traits of Successful Telecommuters" on page 68 are reprinted with permission from *101 Tips for Telecommuters* by Debra A. Dinnocenzo (Berrett-Koehler Publishers, Inc.). The "Supervisor's Checklist for Telecommuters" on page 102 and the "Telecommuter's Agreement" on page 157 are reprinted with permission of the California Department of Personnel Administration. The section from "Moving Telecommuting Forward: An Examination of Organizational Variables" on page 139 is reprinted with permission of the New Jersey Institute of Technology.

The "Meritt Group Telecommute Program," "Meritt Group Cell Phone/Smart Phone Policy," "Remote Access Permission" on pages 165–170, and the Sample Outline on page 98 are used with permission.

Every effort has been made to obtain permission for quoted material. If there is an omission or error, the author and publisher would be grateful to be so informed.

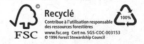

Self-Counsel Press
(a division of)
International Self-Counsel Press Ltd.

1481 Charlotte Road	1704 N. State Street
North Vancouver, BC V7J 1H1	Bellingham, WA 98225
Canada	USA

CONTENTS

Notice   ix

Foreword   xi

Introduction   xv

1   Telecommuting: What It Is and Why You Need to Know   1

Executive Summary   3

   1.   The Origins of Telecommuting   5

   2.   The Terminology of Telecommuting   7

   3.   The Trend toward Telecommuting   9

   4.   The Growth of Telecommuting   10

   5.   Myths and Misconceptions   12

   6.   The Drawbacks and Challenges   14

      6.1   For employers   14

      6.2   For employees   16

   7.   The Benefits and Rewards   17

      7.1   For employers   18

      7.2   For employees   19

   8.   Case Study   22

2 Getting Started   25

    Executive Summary   27

    1. Which Jobs Are Best for Remote Work?   29

    2. Is Your Business Ready to Manage
Off-site Staff?   33

    3. Handling Resistance from Managers
and Employees   35

    4. What Resources Are Required?   37

        4.1 Office equipment and tools   38

        4.2 Safety considerations   39

    5. The Characteristics of a Successful Program   39

    6. Case Study   41

3 Policies And Procedures   43

    Executive Summary   45

    1. Policy Considerations   47

        1.1 Work hours   48

        1.2 Work assignments   48

        1.3 Evaluation   48

        1.4 Salary and benefits   49

        1.5 Overtime   49

        1.6 Equipment   49

    2. Documenting Your Policies and Procedures   49

        2.1 Policy statement   49

        2.2 Selection criteria   51

        2.3 Expectations/responsibilities of off-site employees   51

        2.4 Work schedules   52

        2.5 Equipment and supplies   52

        2.6 Insurance   53

        2.7 Employer's right to inspect workplace   53

        2.8 Privacy and confidentiality   54

        2.9 Performance measurement   54

        2.10 Company policies   54

        2.11 Termination of the agreement   54

        2.12 Employment-at-will disclaimer   55

    3. Case Study   55

4 Off-Site Relationships with Existing Staff   57

Executive Summary   59

1. Working Remotely Is Not for Everyone   62
2. Selection Criteria   63
3. Assessing Candidates   64
4. Traits of Successful Teleworkers   67
5. Perils and Pitfalls   67
   - 5.1 It just doesn't work   67
   - 5.2 It's not fair!   69
   - 5.3 My manager won't let me!   69
6. Case Study   70

5 Recruiting Employees For Telecommuting Positions   71

Executive Summary   73

1. Social media for recruitment   76
2. The Internet as a Recruiting Tool   78
   - 1.2 Effective online recruiting   80
   - 1.3 Using your own website   81
2. Other Sources of Applicants   81
3. Steps in the Hiring Process   82
   - 3.1 Position requirements   83
   - 3.2 Selection criteria   84
   - 3.3 Interviewing candidates for off-site jobs   85
   - 3.4 References   86
4. Perils and Pitfalls   87
5. Case Study   88

6 Training Off-site Workers and Their Managers   91

Executive Summary   93

1. Employee Training   96
   - 1.1 Characteristics of employee training programs   96
   - 1.2 A structure for training   97
   - 1.3 Making it real   99
2. Supervisor/Manager Training   99
   - 2.1 An unnerving transition for managers   100

2.2   A structure for supervisory training   100

2.3   Supervisor's checklist   103

3.   Team Training   103

4.   Training the Rest of the Staff   104

5.   After Training   104

6.   Tips for Starting Telecommuters   105

7.   Case Study   106

7   Managing Telecommuters   109

Executive Summary   111

1.   The Truth about Managing Off-site Staff   113

2.   Traits of Successful Remote Managers   114

3.   Setting Objectives   116

3.1   Establishing job standards   117

3.2   Establishing goals   118

4.   Providing Feedback   120

5.   Communication   121

5.1   The technology of communication   121

6.   Maintaining Involvement   124

7.   Motivating Off-site Staff   125

8.   If the Relationship Doesn't Work   126

9.   Additional Tips for Managers of Off-Site Staff   128

10. Case Study   129

8   Program Outcomes   133

Executive Summary   135

1.   Measuring Program Outcomes   137

2.   Why Alternative Work Arrangements Fail   138

3.   Case Study   141

Appendixes

1. Telecommuting Proposal   145
2. Telecommuting Policy   147
3. Telecommuter's Agreement   157
4. Telecommuting Agreement   159
5. Telecommuting Resources   163
6. Merritt Group Elecommute Program   165
7. Merritt Group Cell Phone/Smart Phone Policy   167
8. Remote Access Permission   169

Tables

1. Percentage of Organizations Offering Various Flexible Working Benefits   21
2. Flexible Work Benefits by Year   22
3. Flexible Work Benefits by Organization Size   22
4. Assessment for Suitability for Telecommuting   65
5. Example of Goals Outlined for Telecommuting Employees   118

Samples

1. Common Traits of Successful Telecommuters   68
2. Examples of Job Recruitment Postings   80
3. Sample Outline for a Telecommuting Training Program   98
4. Teleworking Issues — AG Communication Systems Telework Handbook   130
5. Managing Telecommuters: Tips for Supervisors   131

Figures

1. Barriers to Implementation   35

Checklists

1. Telecommuting Safety Checklist   40
2. Supervisor's Checklist for Telecommuters   102

NOTICE TO READERS

Laws are constantly changing. Every effort is made to keep this publication as current as possible. However, the author, the publisher, and the vendor of this book make no representations or warranties regarding the outcome or the use to which the information in this book is put and are not assuming any liability for any claims, losses, or damages arising out of the use of this book. The reader should not rely on the author or publisher of this book for any professional advice. Please be sure that you have the most recent edition.

FOREWORD

There's a wonderful old Dilbert comic strip in which Dilbert is meeting with the owner of a small business with which Dilbert's firm is forming a strategic alliance. Dilbert comes in with a very thick binder in his hands and tells the other man that the binder contains the procedures his company uses for project management. Dilbert then says, "I guess a small company such as yours is used to flying by the seat of your pants." The small-business owner replies, "Not exactly," prompting Dilbert to ask, "You mean you're flexible?" which draws the reply, "I mean I'm not wearing pants."

When it comes to implementing telecommuting, there is quite a collection of policies, guides, training programs, and all other kinds of resources available in books and on the Web — but most of them are directed at the large organizations that are typical of where telecommuting got its start.

(An aside: It is now time, in my view, to attach an asterisk to the word "telecommuting" or otherwise indicate that we have seen the beginning of the end of "telecommuting" as it was once known. It was a great term when it was coined by Jack Nilles in the mid-1970s but we are, as this book will show you, far beyond the "gee, isn't it cool to be able to work at home" stage. We have, finally, reached the point that

I and many other predicted and hoped for: the day when we begin to simply talk about "work" as an activity without segmenting it according to where it is being done.)

There's nothing wrong with those procedures and manuals — in fact, most of the problems I see when companies try to implement tele-commuting arise when they ignore the practices and knowledge that have developed and accumulated in the last 35 years.

The small-to medium-size organization has, unfortunately, been largely ignored in this scenario. As the Dilbert comic suggests, smaller firms aren't generally as likely to have those six-inch-thick binders and multi-page policies and procedures. But that doesn't mean the smaller firms don't have the need for the same kind of guidance as do the big firms that prepare those behemoth policies.

That's why this book is such an important resource. It bridges the gap between the unique needs of the smaller-business employer and the knowledge base and resources typically available to much larger firms. Most important, this book will inform your thinking about the many ways in which work gets done (and done well) independent of location and, in some cases, independent of organizational boundaries. There really isn't a great deal of difference in how telecommuting can be used in smaller firms — the difference comes about because smaller firms just don't have the internal staff, the time, and the bureaucratic inclinations that make those immense policies work elsewhere. Smaller businesses need the convenience of a field guide. They need this book.

Having been involved in the field of telecommuting* (there's that asterisk, signifying that we all need to wean ourselves from using that word as a transitional crutch) since 1982, I have seen it implemented in virtually every kind of organization — large and small, private sector and public sector, information-intensive and production or service-based, in the US and elsewhere. There are remarkably few differences across this range of firms. The underlying telecommuting concept of se-lectively decentralizing the office — and the business benefits of doing so — are more universal than most people realize.

This book takes those relatively universal experiences and methods and focuses them exclusively on the needs and characteristics of the smaller (but not necessarily small) organization. Lin Grensing-Pophal has done that exceptionally well — and has also packed the book with a range of checklists, sample forms, dos and don'ts, and other practical, easy-to-use tools that will make your job easier.

Let's face it: Organizations that continue to cling to the notion that work can only be done when workers are sitting in the same place at the same time have, or will soon, become antiquated and dysfunctional. We're not going to see offices and office buildings evaporate; what we will see, though, is phenomenally rapid growth in the number of organizations of all sizes that figure out how to enable and guide people to work together without being together.

Implementing off-site staffing in your business can provide excellent opportunities for business growth. You'll find this book to be a well-researched and thorough — yet highly readable and usable — guide to help you decide the best way to implement telecommuting.

Lin Grensing-Pophal has done the entire community of small- and medium-sized organizations a great service by tailoring what we know to this sector of our economy. Take advantage of her hard work and get going!

— Gil Gordon

INTRODUCTION

Even in tight economic times — particularly in tight economic times — business owners want to attract and retain qualified, productive staff members. While rising unemployment rates mean that the availability of workers is greater than it was just a few years ago, the availability of highly skilled and highly motivated workers is always at a premium.

And, of course, as the economy improves and aging baby boomers begin to leave the workforce in droves, it will become harder and harder to find talented and qualified employees. The impact on organizations, large and small, will be considerable. Think of your own workforce and the number of employees who will be eligible for retirement in the near future. Think of the key positions that must remain filled with capable and competent staff in order to ensure quality products and services for your customers.

1. The Need to Retain Employees — Even in a Soft Economy

Most employers will agree that the ability to retain employees, regardless of the economy, is always a critical need. To do this, many are looking for creative ways to meet employee needs. Flexibility is one critical area of demand. For many companies, flexibility means providing the opportunity for employees to telecommute.

In the work environment of the twenty-first century, work is being defined differently than it has ever been defined in the past. The "typical" 9:00 a.m. to 5:00 p.m., Monday-to-Friday work week is a thing of the past. Instead, as jobs have become less structured, work has become less structured in terms of how, when, and where it gets done.

In a global, 24/7 world, the notion that all employees of an organization can work the same rigid schedule is obviously far outdated. Punching a time clock is, in fact, an artifact of the industrial revolution and no longer pertinent for what has largely become a service economy. In addition, today's workers value flexibility more than ever, requiring employers that wish to attract and retain the best and the brightest to come up with flexible solutions to meet their needs.

A survey of human resource managers by the outsourcing services firm, Yoh, indicates that telecommuting is becoming an increasingly important aspect of organizations' ability to recruit and retain top talent. Among the trends identified:

- 25 percent of managers allow working from home, 13 percent allow working from a satellite office, and 44 percent have other arrangements that support telecommuting. Only 19 percent say they have no telecommuting procedure.

- Most managers say they expect telecommuting to grow over the next two years. Only 35 percent said it was unlikely that telecommuting would increase.

- In addition to offering flexibility to desirable workers, telecommuting is growing due to available technologies such as wireless broadband, PDAs, and PCs capable of remote enterprise access.

2. Telecommuting versus Managing Off-site Staff

But while "telecommuting" is a term that has become increasingly familiar and a practice increasingly adopted by companies large and small, the ability to manage off-site staff is really the issue. The first edition of this book focused specifically on telecommuting; this second edition will take a broader look at the issue of managing off-site staff. The principles and practices are really the same — the terminology is just somewhat different. This shift in focus, however, broadens the value of the information in this book. Literally any manager responsible for supervising people who are located "somewhere else" can benefit from the strategies and tactics presented here.

The term "telecommuting" continues to scare many managers. The prospect of being responsible for people who are off-site is often threatening — yet also often entirely misunderstood. Consider, for example, the banking industry, which has multiple branch locations where employees may physically be located, yet they work for a manager who may be located in the corporate office. In my own experience, while working as director of corporate communications for a major, integrated health care facility in the Midwest, I was physically located in a house that had been converted to offices which housed the corporate communications department. The house was near the main facility, but quite removed from the VP I reported to. We maintained contact via phone and email and would occasionally encounter each other at meetings but, the vast majority of time, we were not physically present in the same environment. The truth of the matter was that I could literally have been located anywhere and still performed the requirements of my job to a large degree.

The point here is that telecommuting should not be a concept that is feared. It is an option available to companies today that can add flexibility and value to both employees and managers. In this revised edition we will initially explore the concept of telecommuting and its current status, but will then take a broader approach to the issue of managing off-site staff.

3. Flexible Options, Morale, and Engagement

Providing flexible options for employees remains important for a number of reasons, not the least of which is the impact on morale and "engagement."

The advantages of offering flexibility in work arrangements are attracting more corporate attention, suggests a recent study by the Institute for Corporate Productivity (I4CP). The study found that a full 84 percent of companies overall believe that flexible work arrangements in their organization boosts employee morale. That figure is up from 76 percent in a similar 2008 study conducted by I4CP. Correspondingly, the 2009 study showed that 78 percent of polled companies say flexwork options bolster retention rates, up from 64 percent the previous year.

According to the most recent study results, "flextime" (flexible start/end times) is the most-used flexwork option, with 76 percent of companies overall selecting it as their top option. Working from home was the second-most favored, at 59 percent overall (that figure jumps to 70 percent in companies with more than 10,000 employees), followed by part-time work, pointed to by 56 percent of organizations.

Those most likely to request flexible work arrangements include employees in professional roles (topping the list at 85 percent), followed by those in administrative roles (60 percent). In general, younger employees — 29 percent (41 percent in large companies) — are more likely to request the benefit, and more females (35 percent) than males (6 percent) tend to make such requests.

The most common rationales cited for offering flexible work arrangements by 60 percent of the overall respondents (and 69 percent of large companies) were that the employees, "job doesn't require presence in the office," followed by 60 percent who said long commutes were a reason, and 47 percent of respondents cited offering flexible arrangements for employees returning from maternity leave.

Keeping tabs on flexible work arrangements is also a priority. Sixty-nine percent of polled companies use established deadlines to measure productivity in a flexible work situation, while 66 percent keep an eye on project completion and 39 percent rely on periodic status reports.

With today's added focus on flexwork options, however, come additional concerns. When asked how flexible work options might be a detriment to the organization, almost two-thirds (64 percent) of the 2009 study respondents said that flexwork arrangements tend to frustrate workers who cannot utilize the benefit, compared to 36 percent a year ago, and 42 percent of 2009 respondents reported that the option is frustrating to managers, while just 20 percent felt so in 2008.

Also, the current economic situation appears to have limited bearing on flexwork programs. Sixty percent of all companies polled said the economy has had no effect on their programs, and 19 percent related they have increased flexible work options. Just 8 percent have reduced options in their companies.

4. Changing Employee Needs

The needs of employees have changed dramatically over the past 30 years. Fueled in part by a rapid increase in the number of women entering the workforce, more and more employees are expecting — and demanding — a balance between the expectations of work and the demands of personal life. No longer can managers tell employees to leave their personal lives at home. Today's managers recognize that what happens at home has a dramatic impact on performance at work — and vice versa.

According to the Society for Human Resource Management (SHRM) in their "2008 Employee Job Satisfaction" survey report, 44 percent of employees cited the flexibility to balance work/life issues as a very important aspect of job satisfaction.

The SHRM study further indicated that many companies offer nontraditional scheduling options to employees to help them balance their work and personal lives. Fifty-nine percent of HR professionals indicated their organizations offered flextime, which allowed employees to select their work hours within limits established by the employer. In addition to flextime, 57 percent of human resource professionals indicated that their organizations offered some form of telecommuting: 47 percent of respondents reported that their organizations offered telecommuting on an ad-hoc basis, 35 percent on a part-time basis, and 21 percent on a full-time basis. Thirty-seven percent of HR professionals said their organizations offered compressed workweeks, where full-time employees are allowed to work longer days for part of a week or pay period in exchange for shorter days or a day off during that week or pay period. Eighteen percent of HR professionals reported that their organizations offered job sharing, in which two employees share the responsibilities, accountability and compensation of one full-time job. These types of flexible scheduling benefits allow organizations to recruit and retain motivated workers who may not be able or willing to work a traditional nine-to-five schedule.

Contributing to the change in expectations among employees is the aging of the baby boomer population and the advent of the Gen X and Gen Y (or millennial) employee. Gen X employees include the 46 million people born between 1960 and 1984 (although the exact years vary depending on who you ask). They have been characterized in the media as skeptical and impatient with the status quo, questioning of authority, and fiercely independent. Having witnessed the sacrifices their parents made for their jobs — and the subsequent impacts of staggering job losses in the 1980s and 1990s — they demand a balance between their work lives and home lives. Gen Y employees, generally the children of the baby boomer population, were born between 1977 and 1994 and make up more than 70 million people in the US — about 20 percent of the population. It is the largest generation since the baby boomers.

Gen Y is technologically competent, social-minded and very empowered — they are the offspring of perhaps the most indulgent parents in history. Consequently, they are highly confident and very optimistic about the future. Their expectations may be too high, however, when those expectations butt up against the realities of the workforce. Interestingly, Gen Y is said to be most closely aligned with their baby boomer colleagues, with Gen X in the middle — representing a group that is likely to be less loyal to employers. In fact, the US Labor Department indicates that Gen Xers hold an average of nearly nine different jobs by their thirties. They change jobs in search of new skills, increased responsibility, and new experiences. Their tendency to change positions frequently has had a major impact on the temporary-worker industry.

5. The Impact of Technology

Technology has had a dramatic influence on the workplace and on the ways in which tasks are accomplished. Email, voice mail, and Internet technology mean that employees can literally be in touch with their employer 24 hours a day, 7 days a week. The 24/7 culture is changing the way that employees and employers interact — it is, in fact, changing the very nature of work. Under the old system, employees were tied to the workplace. Tools did not exist to allow contact from remote locations. Today, technology is providing both employers and employees with freedom and flexibility that they would never have imagined even ten short years ago.

Technology is allowing employees to question the status quo and challenge the old ways of doing business. "Why do I need to come to the office to work on a report when I can do it at home on my computer?" "Why can't I access voice mail and email from home?" "Why do I have to be physically located in a phone center to answer customer calls? Why can't I be set up from home to do this?"

And because employers are faced with a shrinking labor market and a growing gap between job seekers' skills and employer needs, more and more are responding to these questions with "Why not?"

What does all this mean? It means that businesses must become more flexible and creative in both the recruitment and retention of employees. It means that the traditional brick-and-mortar workplace will soon give way — in fact, has given way, in many places — to a virtual workplace. It means that neither employees nor employers will be hampered by geographic constraints: An employee can live in Florida and work for a company in Georgia, Wisconsin, California, Ontario, or Saskatchewan.

It means that whether they are telecommuting, or simply working in another location as part of a global organization, branch office or "virtual company," the ability to effectively manage off-site staff is no longer a luxury; it has become a necessity for companies that want to compete effectively in this new millennium.

Chapter 1
TELECOMMUTING: WHAT IT IS AND WHY YOU NEED TO KNOW

Teleworking: "Any form of substitution of information technologies for work-related travel."

Telecommuting: "Moving the work to the workers instead of moving the workers to work."

— Jack Nilles
(a.k.a. "The father of telecommuting")

Executive Summary

What's the difference between teleworking and telecommuting?

There is certainly some confusion around these terms and they are often used incorrectly. Teleworking is a broad term that can be defined as working at a distance. Telecommuting is a form of teleworking, as are satellite offices, neighborhood work centers, and mobile working.

How common is telecommuting?

SHRM's "2008 Employee Job Satisfaction" report indicates that many companies offer nontraditional scheduling options to employees to help them balance their work and personal lives. Fifty-nine percent of HR professionals indicated their organizations offered flextime, which allowed employees to select their work hours within limits established by the employer. In addition to flextime, 57 percent of human resource professionals indicated that their organizations offered some form of telecommuting: 47 percent of respondents reported that their organizations offered telecommuting on an ad-hoc basis, 35 percent on a part-time basis and 21 percent on a full-time basis.

How many teleworkers will there be in the future?

A 2009 study by WorldatWork indicated that the number of US employees who worked remotely at least one day per month increased 39 percent the past two years, from approximately 12.4 million in 2006 to 17.2 million in 2008. In its survey brief Telework Trendlines™ 2009, WorldatWork reports that the sum of all teleworkers — employees, contractors and business owners — has risen 17 percent from 28.7 million in 2006 to 33.7 million in 2008.

What is the biggest barrier to telecommuting?

The greatest barrier may very well be attitude. Managers and companies are often hesitant to consider the option because they fear the loss of control when employees are not located in one place. But the reality of today's workforce is dispersion — satellite offices and international firms mean that even employees who aren't considered telecommuters may be located halfway across the world from their coworkers.

TELECOMMUTING: WHAT IT IS AND WHY YOU NEED TO KNOW

1. The Origins of Telecommuting

As long ago as the nineteenth century, people were telecommuting. While the term wasn't coined until almost 100 years later, the first person on record who performed work at a remote location was a Boston bank president who had a phone line strung from his office to his home — in 1877!

According to Gil Gordon, founder of Gil Gordon Associates (www.gilgordon.com), a management consulting firm specializing in the implementation of telecommuting/virtual office and other alternative work arrangements, the terminology may be new, but the concept really isn't. Gordon is recognized internationally as an expert in the virtual-office concept and is a pioneer in the field. "I've heard stories of people working at home in their living rooms with keypunch in the mid-1960s," Gordon says. But, he points out, telecommuting as we know it can be traced to the late 1970s and early 1980s, when more serious attempts at telecommuting were being made by businesses, and we began to see some widespread adoption of the concept.

Even as early as the 1950s, location was becoming less and less important to the concept of work. Telephone communications were

Telecommuting has been around since 1877, although it did not start to gain widespread popularity until about 100 years later.

widely established. And as the make-up of work changed to a more information-based economy following World War II, staff could work more independently, without need of constant supervision.

You've heard of the Internet, haven't you? Well, in 1963, a programmer working on the Arpanet Project (the forerunner to today's Internet) withdrew from the project to stay home with his wife, who was going through a difficult pregnancy. Another programmer suggested he install an additional phone line in his home so he could program from there. The practice of working from home still didn't have a name, but people were starting to experiment with it.

In 1973, Jack Nilles, a scientist working on a NASA satellite communications projects in Los Angeles, coined the term for telecommuting. Now, Nilles is internationally known as the father of telecommuting. He originally used the term to denote "a geographically dispersed office where workers can work at home on a computer and transmit data and documents to a central office via telephone lines." In 1982, Nilles incorporated JALA International, Inc. (www.jala.com). An international group of management consultants, JALA's mission is "to help organizations make effective use of information technology — telecommunications and computers — and to better cope with the accelerating rate of change in the business environment."

By the time Nilles had come up with a word for the concept of working from locations other than the traditional office, companies were already beginning to experiment with the practice. In 1978, Blue Cross/Blue Shield of South Carolina had started a cottage-keyer project — recognizing that employees could easily perform a number of keyboarding activities at home. In the first year of the project they demonstrated a 26 percent increase in productivity. In 1980, Mountain Bell started a telecommuting project for its managers. That same year the US Army launched a telecommuting pilot.

By the mid-1980s, telecommuting was becoming an increasingly popular option. It seemed to address a number of issues, including gridlock, pollution, employee retention, savings on office space — and even increases in productivity.

In 1989, AT&T started a pilot telecommuting program in Los Angeles; the program was expanded to Phoenix in 1990. Employees tried working at home several days per month. AT&T's move in this direction was a voluntary response to Title I of the 1990 Clean Air Act. In 1992, AT&T introduced a formal telework policy and started its Virtual Workplace training programs. By 1999, more than half of AT&T's managers teleworked at least one day a month; 25 percent of their managers teleworked one day or more per week and 10 percent teleworked 100 percent of the time.

Telecommuting was given a boost in 1990 when amendments to the Clean Air Act mandated employer trip-reduction programs. While telecommuting wasn't a requirement under the Act, it was a recommended way to meet trip-reduction goals and a number of organizations began experimenting with this option. The bill was changed in 1995, and reductions in car-commuter trips are no longer mandatory. However, regional or state rules are still in effect, and telecommuting remains one good way to get cars off the road.

There have been some major changes in telecommuting since its early beginnings. These changes have been driven both by demand and by technology — the Internet, email, and cell phones now make it easier than ever to work from virtually any place, at any time.

In the 1990s, it is estimated that there were approximately 3.7 million workers telecommuting in the United States. In 2000, that number had increased to 6 million. It is estimated that, by the end of 2009, 14 million people will be telecommuting. The rise in these numbers has been driven both by individual and environmental needs.

The entry of Generation Y into the workforce — a demographic that desires flexibility and independence more than those before them — has helped many businesses consider flexible work arrangements as a solution to those desires. Growing concerns for the environment has also spurred an increase in telecommuting as a solution for reducing carbon emissions. The increase in technology options that make it easy — if not seamless — for employees to stay connected regardless of physical location has also had a positive impact.

Flexible working benefits are a cost-effective way to help employees balance their work and personal lives. According to the SHRM 2008 Job Satisfaction survey report, 44 percent of employees cited the flexibility to balance work/life issues as a very important aspect of job satisfaction.

2. The Terminology of Telecommuting

The term "telecommuting" is frequently confused with the term "teleworking." Telework is actually a broad term that includes telecommuting, as well as act of working from satellite offices, neighborhood work centers, and mobile working.

Teleworking means, literally, working from a remote location. The four options mentioned above are all variations of telework.

Telework can be done from home offices, satellite offices, neighborhood work centers, or from no fixed location at all.

Telecommuting refers to employees who work at home on occasion or on a regular basis and who are connected to the workplace through various telecommunications links that might include a telephone, email, or a computer link to office servers. It's the use of information and communication technology to work away from what might be considered the traditional work setting. The most common alternative worksite is the employee's home. Other popular options include telework centers, satellite offices, client offices, hotel rooms, airplanes, trains, and even automobiles.

Satellite offices are facilities that are located at a separate location from the main business headquarters and that house only employees who work for that specific company.

Neighborhood work centers appear to be exactly like satellite offices, but there is one important distinction. While a satellite office would house employees who all work for the same firm, a neighborhood work center includes employees from a variety of different businesses. Neighborhood work centers are most common in large metropolitan areas and provide space for monthly leasing, as well as business equipment such as fax machines and computers.

Mobile workers are employees who really don't have a specific location where they operate. They may frequently be on the road and may use telecommunications technology to keep in contact with their home office. The most common type of mobile worker is a salesperson.

Another commonly used term is hoteling. Hoteling involves assigning office space to employees who come into the office only occasionally. Rather than being assigned a permanent work area, employees who are hoteling make use of a designated area that they may share with others.

Here are Jack Nilles's definitions of teleworking and telecommuting:

Teleworking: Any form of substitution of information technologies (such as telecommunications or computers) for work-related travel.

Telecommuting: Moving the work to the workers instead of moving the workers to work; periodic work out of the principal office for one or more days per week, either at home or in a telework center. The emphasis here is on reduction or elimination of the daily commute to and from the workplace.

And, as Nilles points out, since he coined the terms he should know!

Telecommuting is not the all-or-nothing proposition it is often considered. A teleworker is not necessarily someone who works from home 5 days a week, 52 weeks a year. In fact, according to the International Telework Association & Council (ITAC), the average number of teleworked days is one to two per week.

Whether working at a satellite office, in a neighborhood work center, or at home, the concept of telework is dramatically expanding the options available not only to employees, but to employers around the world.

3. The Trend toward Telecommuting

Telework is a growing work option for companies of all sizes and types. According to the Telework Advisory Group for WorldatWork (ITAC: www.workingfromanywhere.org), there are more than 23.5 million Americans employed by a company who are working from home at least part-time. Just ten years ago in 1999, that figure was 19.6 million — and in 1990, there were just 3.4 million teleworkers in the United States.

Telecommuting can't happen without the support of businesses, but employees themselves are certainly driving the process. Studies show that more and more companies are offering telecommuting and other flexible options as a means of attracting, retaining, and motivating employees.

SHRM's "2008 Employee Job Satisfaction" report indicates that many companies offer nontraditional scheduling options to employees to help them balance their work and personal lives. Fifty-nine percent of Human Resources (HR) professionals indicated their organizations offered flextime, which allowed employees to select their work hours within limits established by the employer. In addition to flextime, 57 percent of HR professionals indicated that their organizations offered some form of telecommuting: Forty-seven percent of respondents reported that their organizations offered telecommuting on an ad-hoc basis, 35 percent on a part-time basis, and 21 percent on a full-time basis. Thirty-seven percent of HR professionals said their organizations offered compressed workweeks, where full-time employees are allowed to work longer days for part of a week or pay period in exchange for shorter days or a day off during that week or pay period. Eighteen percent of HR professionals reported that their organizations offered job sharing, in which two employees share the responsibilities, accountability, and compensation of one full-time job. These types of flexible scheduling benefits allow organizations to recruit and retain motivated workers who may not be able or willing to work a traditional nine-to-five schedule.

A 2009 study by WorldatWork also indicated an increase in telework. The number of US employees who worked remotely (i.e., telecommuted) at least one day per month increased by 39 percent over the past two years, from approximately 12.4 million in 2006 to 17.2 million in 2008. In its survey brief, Telework Trendlines™ 2009, WorldatWork reports that the sum of all teleworkers — employees, contractors, and business owners — has risen by 17 percent, from 28.7 million in 2006 to 33.7 million in 2008.

4. The Growth of Telecommuting

Why is there such tremendous growth in telecommuting now? There are many reasons:

- *Advanced technologies.* The Internet and personal computers have contributed significantly to the ability of people to work from disparate locations. We now have broadband capacity to homes through cable, satellites, fiber-optics, copper wire, and wireless networks; we have improved electronics and communication devices, mobile phones, palmtops, and portable computers; we have sophisticated voicemail systems. All of these factors mean that employees can be just as connected to the workplace from their homes — several hundred miles away — as they are from the office around the corner from the boss.

- *Reduced costs for office space.* In the United States, the federal government found that it could save money on office space — and attract top-notch workers — by allowing employees to telecommute. At Sun Microsystems, where more than 19,000 employees — or 56 percent of the workforce — work away from the office at least once a week, real estate holdings were reduced by 15 percent in 2007. Expenses for employees who work from home at least part of the time range from 30 percent to 70 percent less than those for employees who work in offices.

- *Employee retention.* In an era of double-income families, it is not uncommon for one spouse to accept a job in another location, requiring the other spouse to leave his or her place of employment. Flexible options like telecommuting allow companies to retain spouses who might otherwise need to change employers as part of their relocation. Telecommuting also allows the retention of employees who have family care needs (either for young children or elderly parents), and employees with disabilities who might be difficult to accommodate in the traditional work setting.

A majority of teleworkers at AT&T report increased productivity due to telecommuting, listing fewer meetings and interruptions as reasons.

- *Traffic patterns.* Congestion is often an issue in metropolitan areas. Major events, in some cities, have led to more employers exploring telecommuting options. When Salt Lake City hosted the Olympics in 2002, for instance, preparation for the event meant major road construction and traffic problems. Consequently, a number of employers were more receptive to employees' requests to telecommute. Even in less densely populated areas, travel time can play a role in the move to telecommuting.

- *Environmental issues.* One of the early drivers of the concept of telecommuting, particularly in large, metropolitan areas, was the reduction of air emissions and the elimination of pollution. The federal government in the United States was an early adopter of telecommuting, and President Obama has pledged to expand the option even further under his administration.

- *Employer benefits.* Employers are often initially hesitant to allow employees to telecommute, primarily due to concerns that lack of physical presence will denote lack of involvement on the part of the employee. However, those that have allowed employees to work from home have been surprised to find that productivity actually increases, and employees report higher job satisfaction and improved morale. Alongside reduced real estate costs, many companies have also found that their absenteeism and turnover rates have declined after instituting telecommuting programs.

- *Employee benefits.* Employees enjoy the flexibility of telecommuting as well as the reduced commuting expenses and hassles. They are better able to balance the demands of home and work; they report reduced stress and higher productivity, and demonstrate a strong sense of loyalty and commitment to those organizations that recognize and respond to their personal needs.

Literally thousands of organizations, large and small, have embraced the concept of telework. Some of the companies that have been trailblazers include AT&T, Sun Microsystems, Best Buy, SC Johnson, Yahoo!, Qualcomm, Eli Lilly, and Cisco.

There are many misconceptions surrounding the concept of telecommuting. It's important to investigate these misconceptions with an open mind.

5. Myths and Misconceptions

There are a number of myths and misconceptions associated with telecommuting. Here are a few examples:

Telecommuting is a good idea for women with families, but other employees are unlikely to take advantage of this option. While telecommuting certainly is a positive option for both women and men with young families and can be a great addition to any company's work/life practices, telecommuting should not be considered a child-care option. Employees of both sexes, with or without families, can benefit from telecommuting.

Employees will be too isolated and will become alienated from the team. The fear of isolation is an issue for employees; it is also a concern for employers. Isolation may be a misconception, however. A study by Charles Grantham of the Institute for the Study of Distributed Work indicated that virtual office workers spend 43 percent of their time interacting with other workers. Sixty-one percent reported that they contacted their coworkers two or more times a day, and 94 percent checked in three or more times a week.

While there is certainly potential for isolation when employees are working from remote locations and are not physically located near coworkers, isolation is not a certainty. Much can be done to ensure that there is regular and meaningful contact between the telecommuter and other team members.

If an employee wants to telecommute, they'll be out of the office five days a week. Telecommuting isn't necessarily an all-or-nothing proposition. While some employees do literally work in a remote location eight hours a day, five days a week, arrangements are varied and dependent upon the employee's — and the employer's — unique needs. In fact, according to Telecommute America, a nonprofit organization that promotes telecommuting, telecommuters work an average of only 19.3 hours a week from home.

If I let one employee telecommute, I'll have to let all employees have the opportunity. Not every job is appropriate for telecommuting and neither is every employee. Jobs, for example, that require frequent face-to-face interaction with internal or external customers are obviously not right for telecommuting. Similarly, employees who require direct supervision or who have not demonstrated a high level of competency would not be good candidates for such an arrangement.

The bottom line is that the decision must be made by the company and by the manager. With a telecommuting program, you make no guarantees that everyone can be a telecommuter. Part of the process is establishing clear guidelines, standards, and policies.

Everyone will want to telecommute and there will be nobody left in the office. Just as you may not want certain employees to telecommute, you will have employees who prefer the standard workplace environment. Many employees enjoy the social aspects of work. They like the interactions with others, and the opportunity to leave home and enter a different environment. For those people, telecommuting is unlikely to become a preferred option. As a manager, you are in control of how you staff your department. There are some managers of workforces comprised entirely of telecommuters — in fact, the manager may be a telecommuter too. There are others who, for whatever reasons, do not find that telecommuting is a viable option. And there are many, many more who find that the right solution is somewhere in between. Ultimately, though, you are responsible for staffing your workforce to provide the optimum service to your internal and external customers.

Only big companies are involved in telecommuting. Not true. In fact, a survey by Telecommute America showed that 65 percent of the respondents that participated in telecommuting were from companies with fewer than 100 employees. Telecommuting runs the gamut from small firms with only a handful of employees to multi-national firms. It's not size that matters — it's process and service.

It is too difficult to manage telecommuters. In fact, telemanagers and the companies they work for consistently say that good managers are good managers, regardless of whether they're managing someone in the office or from a remote location. The skills are the same.

6. The Drawbacks and Challenges

Even though the time is right for telecommuting, there are a number of drawbacks and challenges of which both organizations and individuals need to be aware.

6.1 For employers

Resistance to change. Telecommuting has been driven largely by employees who, because of their unique personal needs, have requested flexible options for accomplishing their duties. While some employers were early adopters of telecommuting as a work option, and while studies continue to show that more and more companies are offering employees the opportunity to telecommute, many have been resistant to change. Some employers see no need to change a system that has worked for decades and, as most of us can relate to, change can be personally and organizationally challenging.

Out of sight, out of mind. Front-line managers have tended to be the most resistant to the use of telecommuting as an employee option. They believe that employees who are not physically present will be impossible to oversee. "How can I tell whether they're really working?" they ask. "I'm just not comfortable with the idea of letting employees work from home," others say.

Consider, though, how often managers actually oversee the work of their employees in a traditional setting. Managers may be physically located in an area removed from their staff. They may be involved in numerous meetings and other activities throughout the day that preclude direct observation of employees. And, of course, they have their own work to do, meaning that it is very unlikely that they are actually observing employees in the workplace to any great degree.

Abuse of the option. Are there employees who will take advantage of the opportunity to work from home? Employees who may look at telecommuting as a way of saving money and childcare costs while allowing them plenty of time for interaction with the kids? Employees who will spend their time engaged in personal activities instead of concentrating on their assigned work responsibilities? Certainly. But these individuals would be non-productive in any type of setting. A good selection process will serve to screen out these individuals before they are able to take part in a telecommuting program. In addition, careful development of specific — and measurable — goals and objectives can provide management with an objective method of monitoring performance.

Telecommuting demands greater coordination. Companies may be hesitant to start a telecommuting program because they fear that it will demand greater coordination and require more time and effort than the management of traditional staff. This may be true initially as the program is being developed and as the organization is adapting to it. In the long run, however, telecommuting can strengthen all management practices by helping the organization focus more on outcome than process in the management of staff activities.

Telecommuting may have a negative impact on communication. Communication is certainly a challenge when employees are no longer physically located with the majority of their workgroup and when you can't simply walk down the hall to interact. Communication is a challenge in any work setting, however, and as with the coordination of work activities, the communication needs driven by telecommuting may serve to improve communication overall within the organization.

Special communication challenges are not unique to telecommuting. Many companies operate globally today, with employees spread around the world. Communication is an issue that belongs to any organization.

Fortunately, the technology that is now readily available to virtually anyone (at a very reasonable cost) means that distance is no longer relevant.

Legal issues. All employers have legal rights and responsibilities with respect to their employees; telecommuting simply creates different issues. For example, one of the largest areas of concern is for the safety of employees in a home office, or worker's compensation. Another concern that may develop is the one of wage and hour laws (i.e., when will the telecommuter be eligible for overtime pay?).

These are valid concerns and, fortunately, with the growing number of people and companies practicing telecommuting, the vast majority of legal concerns have been explored and tested by someone, someplace, at some time. The best bits of advice in this area are: spend adequate time preparing your telecommuting agreement; include those issues that may create problems; and obtain legal counsel.

Conflict between teleworkers and non-teleworkers. Telecommuting is not appropriate for all people. Your decision on whether or not to allow an employee to telecommute is likely to be based both on the requirements of the job and the individual characteristics of the employee. Working from home or from some other remote location is an attractive option, and it is not unlikely that the employees who are

Telecommuting raises some interesting legal issues, such as workers' compensation and overtime pay.

Employees may be hesitant to try telecommuting, fearing that they may have difficulty advancing in their careers if they are less visible.

unable to take advantage of it will feel some resentment toward those who are. Conflict may escalate if communication or hand-offs become problematic.

As a manager, it is important to remain focused on the business imperatives of the telecommuting decision.

Initial cost of set-up. Some people may be opposed to telecommuting because of concern over the costs involved. Costs will, of course, vary depending on the job that needs to be done, but generally speaking, it should cost no more to set up an employee to work from home than it does to accommodate the employee at the normal work setting. In fact, many companies have documented substantial savings in office space and equipment needs.

Careful planning is the key to controlling costs, as is common sense. A telecommuter may have the need to make photocopies from time to time, but that does not necessarily mean that he or she should be provided with a photocopier for his or her home office.

Negative impact on teamwork. There is something to be said about the camaraderie that develops between a group of people working together, day after day, within the same work environment. And it can certainly be challenging for a manager to build and maintain that same sense of team when some of the team members are seemingly absent. But it can be done.

6.2 For employees

Not all employees are anxious to telecommute. In fact, employees harbor a number of fears about telecommuting. As a manager it is important that you understand some of these concerns and that you're able to directly and candidly discuss them with staff members. There are disadvantages to telecommuting and, for some employees, these disadvantages can be insurmountable.

Isolation. One of the real benefits of working at the office is the social interaction with other people. While any telecommuter should have ample opportunity for communication with the head office — through email, phone, video conference, and in-person meetings — the fact remains that a lot of time will be spent alone. While some employees may thrive in this type of environment, others may find the isolation difficult to deal with.

Home distractions. People working from their homes often have difficulty creating an appropriate boundary between home and work. Friends, family, and neighbors may perceive that the at-home employee is more receptive to drop-in visits, phone calls, and other interruptions.

Telecommuters whose arrangements allow them to work with their children present have other distractions. And, of course, there are the distractions that telecommuters create for themselves: the temptations of nice, sunny days; the lure of the television; the unrelenting desire to throw in a load of laundry.

Workaholism. The difficulty of drawing a distinction between home and work may create a problem of over-dedication to the job. Telecommuters are often tempted to work longer hours and can find it difficult to create appropriate boundaries between work responsibilities and personal needs. When the office is always just steps away, the lure of completing a project, checking email, or doing just one more thing can be strong.

Limited access to copiers, fax, and other office services. While you will want to consider carefully each telecommuter's needs in terms of work equipment and tools, depending on the employee and his or her job, you may not be able to justify providing every piece of office equipment available for the home office. An employee may need to rely on administrative assistance at the head office or plan occasional trips into the office to take care of routine tasks.

Invisibility — a career killer? Employees may be hesitant to pursue telecommuting because they have come to view it as a career killer. They fear that if they aren't continually involved, they will be overlooked for key projects, assignments, and promotions. This is a very real concern. However, a 1997 survey of telecommuters showed that 63 percent felt that teleworking had been a positive influence on their careers, and only 3 percent reported any negative impact.

Typically, it is the most independent and self-motivated individuals who are good candidates for telecommuting — the same traits that characterize upwardly mobile employees in general. As a manager, one of your key responsibilities is employee development. Telecommuters, as part of the staff, need to be part of this process.

Telecommuting can benefit both employers and employees in a variety of ways.

7. The Benefits and Rewards

There are certainly potential barriers to making telecommuting work and there are some disadvantages for both employees and employers. There are also, however, a number of very definite advantages; there are good reasons why so many individuals and companies are turning to telecommuting as a work option.

SHRM's "2008 Employee Job Satisfaction" report indicated that 46 percent of employees cited the flexibility to balance work/life issues as a very important aspect of job satisfaction. Many companies currently offer nontraditional scheduling options to employees to help them balance their work and personal lives. In fact, 54 percent of the HR professionals responding to the survey indicated that their organizations offered flextime, allowing employees to select their work hours within limits established by the employer. In addition to flextime, 51 percent indicated that their organizations offered some form of telecommuting: 45 percent on an ad-hoc basis, 34 percent on a part-time basis and 19 percent on a full-time basis. Clearly both employers and employees are seeing benefits and rewards associated with telecommuting and other flextime options.

7.1 For employers

Improved productivity. While there are some who question the productivity gains espoused by companies that offer telecommuting options to employees, most will claim a positive impact. The Gartner Group has estimated productivity improvements from 10 percent to 40 percent. Nortel, with more than 4,000 telecommuters, reports productivity improvements of 24 percent since 1995 — with an associated 10 percent increase in job satisfaction and reduced turnover risk of 24 percent.

Reduced sick time. Employers find that telecommuters have fewer sick days — an average of one to two days a year. It makes sense. There are times when a cold may make the thought of spending the day at the office seem like torture, but you might be perfectly able to function at home.

Reduction in office space costs. IBM has reported $75 million in annual savings on real estate expenses because of their telecommuting program. AT&T estimates that its implementation of teleworking results in an average savings of $25 million per year.

Environmental concerns. While the US Clean Air Act was changed in 1995 and no longer makes reductions in car-commuter trips mandatory, and further environmental laws may be forthcoming, environmentally aware employers know that telecommuting can have a positive impact on traffic congestion and, ultimately, emissions.

Weather and other traffic-related concerns. In Atlanta, companies began implementing telecommuting during the summer Olympics of 1996 when traffic, related not only to the event but also to event preparation, created difficulties for commuters. In northern climates, telecommuting means that snow days are a thing of the past. When you have only to commute on foot from one room to another in your house, bad weather is no longer a barrier.

Broader talent pool. The labor pool has experienced some significant fluctuations over the past few years. It is sometimes difficult to find skilled, qualified, and motivated employees. Telecommuting (and the technology that goes with it) makes it possible to bypass the boundaries of geography. For employers, that means the ability to select from a much broader pool of talent. It also means that barriers are removed when, for instance, a merger means that corporate headquarters moves to a new location and a number of highly skilled employees, unable or unwilling to relocate, now have the option of continuing to work for the company, but from their homes.

Enhanced opportunities for disabled individuals. Telecommuting provides a workable and effective way to accommodate employees with various health problems and disabilities that might otherwise keep them out of the labor market. Far beyond complying with legal regulations, the option of telecommuting can allow employers to provide highly qualified but disabled employees with the opportunity to contribute their talents toward meaningful endeavors.

Improved attractiveness of company to job candidates. Employees are, more than ever, giving their personal lives precedence over their professional lives. To many, the ability to work in a flexible environment is very attractive. Even those employees who are not interested in telecommuting may perceive a company that offers the option as being progressive and concerned with meeting the needs of its employees.

Move toward management by results. All managers should manage like managers of telecommuters. By focusing on results, managers can let go of outmoded ideas of employee surveillance or concern about the number of hours that an employee puts in. What matters are the outcomes. Today's successful managers work collaboratively with their employees, recognizing that the measurement of performance depends more on quantitative results than subjective perceptions of an employee's hard work.

7.2 For employees

Reduced or eliminated commute time. In major metropolitan areas and even in some smaller communities, a daily commute may mean putting up with traffic, congestion, long wait times, and frustration. Telecommuting eliminates these concerns — and allows employees to save money on gasoline, vehicle maintenance, and other travel-related costs.

The elimination of a one-hour, round-trip commute each day results in a savings of six full weeks of work per year.

Flexibility. Formerly, employees were confined to their work areas from a certain time in the morning until a certain time in the afternoon, for a specific number of days each week. They were generally allowed one break in the morning and one in the afternoon (both at pre-determined times) and a lunch period of anywhere from 15 minutes to an hour. To put it simply, their time was rigidly controlled and governed by the needs (or, more precisely, the whims) of their employers.

As employees have become more independent and the employment options available to them have increased, they have begun to question this rigidity and to request — even demand — flexibility in how their time is scheduled. Telecommuting responds to these requests by recognizing that it is no longer a 9-to-5 world. Today's employees, if provided with the appropriate work tools and communication channels, can effectively work any time during the 24-hour day — 7 days a week.

An environment free of disruptions. The workplace can be very distracting and may result in lost productivity. Telecommuters frequently report (and companies agree) that they are more productive because they have greater privacy and fewer unplanned interruptions of their time.

Ability to balance work and home demands. Telecommuters are better able to balance the demands of work with the demands and personal needs of their home lives. Raising young children, caring for older parents, pursuing hobbies and personal interests; all this can be accomplished with less stress and frustration when the traditional concept of work is changed to one that recognizes the needs of the whole employee.

Decrease in miscellaneous expenses (i.e., clothing, meals). As any employee knows, there are a lot of miscellaneous expenses associated with working, including transportation costs, clothing, and food. Telecommuters are able to save on these costs, which results in a positive impact on their disposable income.

Elimination of transportation problems. Telecommuting eliminates travel concerns for employees in areas where winter can mean snowy and icy roads — and days when they simply can't safely get to work.

While the many misconceptions associated with telecommuting can certainly keep companies from moving toward this flexible option, the biggest factor that limits the use of telecommuting at many companies is trust. Embarking on a telecommuting program can require a major paradigm shift for many organizations and individuals. Rather than believing that you are paying an employee for his or her time, you must move to an understanding that you are really paying an employee for his or her output — whether that output is measured in number of sales, completion of specific projects, or consultation.

Telecommuting means that we no longer have to go where the work is. Today, the workplace has become more of a concept than a place.

However, telecommuting is just one iteration of a concept that is and has been widespread for years — that of managing off-site staff. Whether in a formal telecommuting arrangement as part of a virtual company, while working with off-site contractors, or while managing employees who may be located at different company sites or branches, the best practices in selecting employees, developing policies and procedures, monitoring progress, and — most importantly — communicating effectively, are remarkably consistent. As we proceed through the rest of this book, the focus will primarily be on managing off-site staff in any of these situations. The term "telecommuting" will be used only to specifically address formal telecommuting programs as outlined in this chapter. Chapter 5 will also focus specifically on telecommuting and address hiring staff specifically for telecommuting positions.

Carol Stein of HR Library successfully convinced management to let her telecommute. She stresses the importance of having a "very precise plan" before requesting or attempting to telecommute.

TABLE 1
PERCENTAGE OF ORGANIZATIONS OFFERING VARIOUS FLEXIBLE WORKING BENEFITS

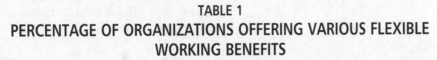

	% Currently offering	% Offering, but planning to reduce or eliminate	% Not offering, but planning to w/in the next 12 months
Flextime	54	1	0
Telecommuting: ad hoc	45	1	0
Compressed workweek	37	1	0
Telecommuting: part-time	34	2	0
Shift flexibilty	21	3	0
Telecommuting: full-time	19	1	*
Job Sharing	16	2	*
Seasonal scheduling	16	1	1
Alternating location arrangements	4	9	0

* Less than 1%

Source: 2009 Employee Benefits: A Survey Report by SHRM

TABLE 2
FLEXIBLE WORK BENEFITS BY YEAR

	2005 (%)	2006 (%)	2007 (%)	2008 (%)	2009 (%)
Flextime	56	57	58	59	54
Telecommuting: ad hoc	—	45	48	47	45
Compressed workweek	33	35	38	37	37
Telecommuting: part-time	37	26	33	35	34
Shift flexibilty	—	—	—	26	21
Telecommuting: full-time	19	19	21	21	19
Job Sharing	19	18	20	18	16
Seasonal scheduling	—	—	—	—	16
Alternating location arrangements	—	—	—	—	4

Source: 2009 Employee Benefits: A Survey Report by SHRM

TABLE 3
FLEXIBLE WORK BENEFITS BY ORGANIZATION SIZE

	Overall	Small (1-99 employees)	Medium (100-499 employees)	Large (500+ employees)
Flextime	54	58	46	66
Telecommuting: ad hoc	45	43	39	54
Compressed workweek	37	38	31	45
Telecommuting: part-time	34	29	26	47
Shift flexibilty	21	13	25	24
Telecommuting: full-time	19	17	13	31
Job Sharing	16	8	13	29
Seasonal scheduling	16	8	14	22
Alternating location arrangements				

Source: 2009 Employee Benefits: A Survey Report by SHRM

8. Case Study

Amanda Vega of Amanda Vega Consulting (www.amandavega.com), with headquarters in Arizona, manages on-site and off-site staff. Her company has offered public relations and social media services to clients nationally and globally for many years. "We deal with multiple languages and different countries and take into consideration the different cultures we work with," says Vega.

The first office was established in New York City and currently employs eight full-time employees who spend about 50 percent of their time on-site, says Vega. "Most of these were high-paid advertising executives at big firms that we were able to hire at a lower salary because of the flexibility we offer," she says.

Vega says it was natural for her to set up her company as a virtual organization to a large degree because she had worked virtually with AOL for a number of years. But, having enjoyed the virtual work experience, Vega found it hard to adjust when she was asked to transition to AOL's home office in Silicon Valley. "That was very weird for me," she says.

She prefers a virtual work existence and established her company to allow flexibility for her and her staff. But flexibility doesn't mean lack of accountability.

Vega monitors performance and holds staff accountable through specific expectations, frequent communication and tools that allow her to manage projects and remain continually up-to-date on progress. "We have one standard Excel file that has all clients listed, who the account manager is and what the deliverables are," she says. Monday morning conference calls provide an opportunity for formal updates on progress. Ongoing communication occurs through phone, email, and social media tools like Twitter.

Vega notes that she can demand high performance and accountability from her staff because of the value they place on the ability to have flexible work arrangements — and because there are so many others out there who would love to take their place! "People love to work from home," she says.

"I'm not sure that businesses have really thought about this, but you're giving employees an incredible luxury by allowing this flexibility," says Vega. The ability to work off-site, she says, is a benefit that employees highly appreciate but which doesn't cost an employer much to provide. A win-win for both sides.

Chapter 2
GETTING STARTED

*"You can do any idea you want from anywhere you want
with the available technology and the new attitudes
people have about collaboration."*

— Jennifer Johnson
Founder of virtual agency Johnson & Company

Executive Summary

What types of jobs are best suited for remote work?

There are a wide variety of jobs — or portions of jobs — that can be performed in locations other than a corporate headquarters or company office. As flexible scheduling has become more widespread, more and more companies and their employees are exploring creative ways of offering flexible work arrangements, whether through modifications in work schedules or work locations. Traditionally, the types of jobs that have been most suited to nontraditional scheduling are those that require limited face-to-face contact with coworkers. But today, advances in technology and adjustments in attitude mean that a wide range of people have been able to work from virtually anywhere, any time.

How much does it cost to allow flexible scheduling options?

That depends. It depends upon the type of job being done, the number of people working as telecommuters, and their equipment and communication needs. Costs can vary widely. Hewlett-Packard and Pacific Bell have reported average costs per employee of $4,000 to $6,000 per year for their telecommuting staff; but remember, your actual costs will depend on the type of work being done and the equipment and technology needs of your home-based employees.

What is the best response to an employee's request for flexible scheduling?

It is best to consider flexible options before requests are made by individual employees. The decision to allow employees to work off-site or to have flexible schedules should optimally be based upon the needs and characteristics of the job — not the personal needs of the employee. However, many organizations do not consider these options until a valued employee is lost due to relocation. The best response to any request is to carefully consider the impact on the organization and its customers and employees.

Who should be responsible for providing equipment for an employee's use at home?

There are a number of benefits to the employer in providing the equipment that employees will use. Primary among these is control. If it's your equipment, you are able to indicate what type of equipment the employee should have, and to determine how that equipment is used and when it is serviced and upgraded. Employer-owned equipment may also be wise from a safety and security standpoint, particularly if the employee will have access to sensitive customer or company data.

GETTING STARTED

Perhaps you already have a telecommuting program in place and are looking for ways to make the program more efficient, more effective, or more equitable across the organization. Maybe an employee has asked you about the option of arranging for more flexible work hours. Perhaps your organization has multiple sites and you're finding that managers and supervisors are more and more frequently called upon to manage staff that are not located where they are.

Regardless of your motivation, it's best to be proactive rather than reactive. Before an employee surprises you with a proposal, or simply asks, "Can I work from home?" you should consider the pros and cons and determine what your organization's policies and procedures will be.

1. Which Jobs Are Best for Remote Work?

There are certain types of jobs that have involved working from remote or off-site locations for years. Salespeople, for instance, have traditionally operated out of places other than a typical office setting. They may work on the road or they may work from their homes. Freelance writers for major magazines work from their homes or from remote locations, and are often not physically located in the office, or even in the city,

There are a number of factors to consider when deciding whether telecommuting would be appropriate for a particular job.

where the magazine is located. Telemarketers often do not require a centralized location, but may operate virtually from their homes or satellite centers. As long as they have the communication equipment and computer information they need to sell the company's products and services, where they sell it really doesn't make a difference. And more recently, the computer industry has spawned some major growth in the prevalence and acceptance of employees located at remote sites for a variety of positions.

There are also certain jobs that may require the employee to be physically on-site. Some obvious examples are waiters and waitresses, bank tellers, and check-out clerks in grocery stores or retail settings. With the rapid changes being made in technology and in the way we view work, however, and with some creative solutions, even some of these jobs may eventually be appropriate for off-site work. For instance, not that long ago, most people would have said that teachers could not be located outside of the classroom setting — they had to be face-to-face with their students. Today, technology has made it possible for students to take courses online, meaning that the teacher and the students can all be located in different places. Similarly, many people still feel that management positions are not appropriate for working in locations separate from staff members, yet even management staff have been able to take advantage of telecommuting options. And, as we've already discussed, it is highly common for managers in certain industries and in global settings to manage employees remotely.

For companies considering a formal telework program, there are certain kinds of jobs that are most suitable for these arrangements. SHRM's "2008 Employee Job Satisfaction" survey indicated that the most common rationales cited for offering flexible work arrangements by 60 percent of the overall respondents (and 69 percent of large companies) were that the employees' job "doesn't require presence in the office." Sixty percent said that long commutes were among their reasons for offering telework, and 47 percent of respondents cited offering flexible arrangements for employees returning from maternity leave as among their reasons. The types of jobs that are most appropriate for telecommuting arrangements include:

(a) Jobs that involve more telephone interaction than face-to-face interaction. A great many phone centers and telemarketing operations utilize telecommuters; in fact, telephone interactions are probably one of the best examples of a job that is dependent on the availability of technology.

(b) Jobs that can be evaluated primarily by quantitative rather than qualitative results. Results are what count when managing telecommuters — not the amount of time spent in the office. Sales positions are a good example of a type of job in which results dictate success.

(c) Jobs that do not involve high security or handling of proprietary data. Data security is a major issue and is becoming more and more important as technology continues to make the sharing of data easier. In the health-care field, for example, confidentiality of patient information is a major issue.

(d) Information-handling jobs that require computers (i.e., insurance, accounting, programming, data entry, design).

(e) Individual-contributor jobs not dependent on a team environment to accomplish tasks. Examples might include freelance writers, graphic designers, consultants of various types, and, often, computer programmers.

Some job functions that are suited to telecommuting include —

- data entry,
- typing,
- computer programming,
- research,
- writing,
- editing,
- graphic design,
- report preparation and analysis, and
- record keeping.

Of course, there is room for interpretation and flexibility within your own establishment, but the suggestions listed here can form the foundation of any telecommuting program.

The US federal government takes an interesting approach to eligibility for its telework opportunities. Rather than focusing on who can take advantage of telework opportunities, it focuses on who can't. All federal employees are considered eligible unless:

- Positions require, on a daily basis (every work day), direct handling of secure materials or on-site activity that cannot be handled remotely or at an alternate site, such as: face-to-face personal contact in medical, counseling, or similar services; hands-on contact with machinery, equipment, vehicles, etc.; or other physical presence/site-dependent activity such as forest ranger or guard duty tasks; or

- Last federal government performance rating on record (or its equivalent) is below fully successful or conduct has resulted in disciplinary action within the last year.

Based on these guidelines, Federal agencies identified two-thirds (more than 1 million) of employees were eligible for telework. Those not eligible were employees whose positions required daily on-site activity. For instance, at the Transportation Security Administration (TSA) only 64 of approximately 60,000 employees telework. Only 3 of approximately 6,500 Secret Service employees telework.

The telecommunications giant Sprint has a very formalized process for determining whether or not a position is appropriate for telecommuters. The people at Sprint have created a company handbook that walks managers through the selection process.

Five major areas are considered:

1. The job itself

2. The function that the person is performing

3. The individual's interaction with the workgroup

4. Space and equipment requirements

5. Information security requirements

Management is asked to rate each item according to a scale on which **a** meets all the requirements and **e** is not a good selection.

Over time and through experience, Sprint has been able to identify certain types of jobs that fall into each of the categories from **a** to **e**:

(a) Internal audit functions, events management, training and development, processing operations, and outside sales.

(b) Positions that may require technology beyond what a typical user would have in the office — specific positions might include systems developers, programmers, producers, or directors.

(c) Positions that provide support to the organization such as field staff, marketing services, regulatory and government affairs, and some engineering functions.

(d) Positions that Sprint feels are almost impossible to perform away from the workplace, including: human resources, corporate communications, public relations, inside sales, end-user support, customer service, operator service, and safety.

(e) Positions that are considered definitely not appropriate for telecommuting; treasury, procurement, controller and accounting functions, strategic planning and development, law, warehouse distribution, and corporate security.

Be sure to clearly outline company policies on work hours, work assignments, evaluation, salary and benefits, overtime, and equipment.

Remember that these criteria are specific to Sprint. Other organizations may — and often do — consider some of Sprint's category **d** and **e** positions appropriate for telecommuting. The key is to carefully review your organization's needs, your job functions, and the specific criteria that will determine whether a specific position is appropriate to be performed off-site.

These methods of assessment may provide a good starting point for your telecommuting program, but you will have to adapt your policy to suit the needs of your business. Don't make your decisions in a vacuum. Involve other members of the organization — and even your customers — in the decision-making process. Developing a dialogue to consider these issues will not only help you make an informed decision, but will ease some of the concerns and misconceptions that other employees and managers may have.

2. Is Your Business Ready to Manage Off-site Staff?

Companies most effective in managing workers who are located off-site share a number of characteristics, which are outlined below.

Commitment and support from management. If yours is a small, independently owned business managed primarily by you, you can move forward with various flexible work options with few problems. The larger your business and the more management staff involved, however, the more work that needs to be done to encourage commitment and support from management. Managing remote workers will not be as effective if policies, practices, and processes are applied inconsistently throughout the organization — for example, if one manager permits an employee to work from home one day a week, but another refuses to consider the option.

Selection at the department level. Individual managers and supervisors need to be responsible for selecting the positions and individuals that should — or could — be located off-site. This is part of managing a department. While the rules and criteria should be applied consistently from an overall business level, it is important that actual selection of telecommuting positions and individuals occurs at the department level. In some cases, the decisions will be obvious. Credit unions need to staff branch locations with personnel that may report in to an administrator in the main location. Similarly, health-care organizations may have administrative positions located throughout a wide geography to serve individual clinic or hospital locations.

Clear guidelines. Clear guidelines are key, particularly when decisions are being made more for personal preference than business necessity. Guidelines should be carefully considered, thoroughly documented and communicated, and consistently applied. Chapter 3 provides more detail on developing guidelines and offers sample guidelines and language that can be modified to fit your business needs. The guidelines will indicate to employees and managers what criteria are needed for approving off-site work arrangements, how employees might request consideration for these opportunities and what the requirements are for ongoing participation. Consistency in the application of these guidelines is important. The SHRM "Employee Job Satisfaction" report indicated that almost two-thirds (64 percent) of the 2009 study respondents said that flexwork arrangements tend to frustrate workers who cannot utilize the benefit, compared to 36 percent a year ago. Forty-two percent of 2009 respondents reported that the option is frustrating to managers, while just 20 percent felt so in 2008.

A contract/agreement outlining the variance in work relationship. Particularly in more formal telecommuting situations, a contract or agreement can avoid misunderstandings and ensure that the organization and employee are on the same wavelength when it comes to the nitty-gritty details of the modified work arrangement. Items to be included in the contract include: hours the employee is expected to be available by phone or email, times the employee will need to report to the office, equipment that will be provided by the employer, safety issues, performance expectations, and training. See Chapter 3 for more information.

Training for both staff and managers. The training of off-site staff, particularly telecommuters, and their managers is essential. Simply providing an employee with a computer and email is not enough. You may also want to consider providing training for those employees who will still be operating out of the office. The more you can do to thoroughly prepare the individuals involved in — or impacted by — flexible work arrangements, the greater your likelihood of success. Chapter 6 provides detailed information on establishing training programs.

A method of evaluation. How will you know if a modified work arrangement is successful? Establishing clear criteria to evaluate success against pre-determined goals — for both the employee and the organization — will help determine if the time and effort invested is achieving desired results.

3. Handling Resistance from Managers and Employees

As the SHRM study suggests, not all employees or your managers are going to eagerly embrace the concept of flexible work arrangements. Many employees, particularly those that have been on the job for a number of years and have grown comfortable with a particular way of working, may feel threatened by the changes that this flexibility may bring, primarily in terms of their ability to interact regularly with fellow employees in the manner they're used to.

The Status of Telework in the federal government report, created by the U.S. Office of Personnel Management in December of 2008, gathered input from 80 Executive Branch agencies and provided an overview of the status of telework in the federal government from January 1 through December 31, 2007. The chart below indicates respondents' perspectives on the primary barriers to implementation of telework.

FIGURE 1
BARRIERS TO IMPLEMENTATION

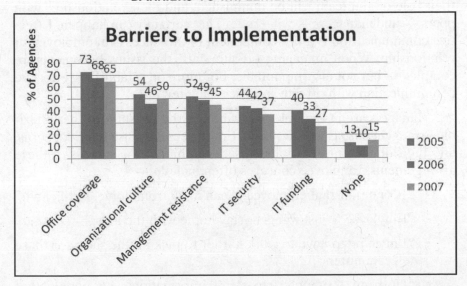

The best way to respond to resistance is to understand where the resistance is coming from and what issues are creating concerns. Some of the concerns are predictable and, as we saw in Chapter 1, there are a number of myths and misconceptions that you can clarify with employees.

For managers, concerns often center around issues such as —

- "How can I supervise someone who is not in the office?"

- "How will I know if these employees are really working?"

- "Is it worth my time and effort to institute the guidelines and tracking systems necessary to make this work?"

These are legitimate questions, and it is important that you take the time to seriously listen to the concerns of your management staff and work out any problems.

The idea of supervising employees who are not physically accessible can be troublesome to managers who are used to having employees within view at all times. It is a different way of managing, but it is not an insurmountable problem. We will be discussing methods of managing telecommuting or off-site staff in Chapter 7.

Another very legitimate concern that managers have about off-site employees is that they will be out of sight, and therefore out of mind. Managers are concerned that employees working away from the main physical location will miss out on critical information because they are no longer part of the informal communication channel, that their role on the team will be diminished, and their relationships with peers — and managers — will erode. That certainly can happen. Effective communication is a key component of any successful employment relationship. When managing off-site staff, the issues become more complex — but not insurmountable. For more on establishing effective communication with off-site staff, see Chapter 7.

Managers aren't the only ones who may be resistant to these flexible arrangements, as we have seen. Employees may also have concerns, and their discontent, if not addressed, can hinder the success of these arrangements. Employee concerns often include —

- "It's not fair that employee X can work from home, but I can't."

- "Employee Y just wants to stay home with the kids."

- "I'm going to have to work harder to pick up the slack for these telecommuters."

- "How am I supposed to share information with people that aren't even around?"

There is an inherent benefit implied in the ability to work off-site, especially if that site is the employee's own home. Employees who are given this opportunity may elicit envy from their coworkers who, for whatever reasons, are not able to have the same flexibility. It is important to recognize the potential for internal conflict and jealousy. To minimize these conflicts, it is necessary to have very clearly identified, defined, and communicated criteria for the arrangement. Consistently adhering to these criteria can help to minimize conflict and jealousy among employees.

Frequent communication is an excellent way to overcome misconceptions that employees may have about their off-site peers. The concern that a new mother just wants to spend time at home with the baby, for instance, can be minimized by communicating the goals of the position and sharing information about the attainment of those goals. For example, if an off-site employee is part of a workgroup that is responsible for handling insurance claims, holding each employee (off-site and on-site) accountable for a specific number of claims can eliminate concerns about how time is being spent in a home location, for instance.

Resistance to change can be most readily overcome by implementing a well-defined system of policies and procedures with which everyone can become quickly familiar.

4. What Resources Are Required?

The cost for setting up a home office for an employee can vary dramatically, as you might imagine. Different jobs will, of course, require different tools, and different companies have different capabilities. Who, then, should supply what? It seems that this, too, varies from business to business. Brad and Debbie Shepp, authors of *The Telecommuter's Handbook* (McGraw-Hill), surveyed 100 telecommuting companies and found that 48 percent supplied all of the necessary equipment for telecommuters. Another 26 percent shared the equipment expense with their telecommuters. Pacific Bell budgeted $4,000 per person, per year, for home-office needs, while Hewlett-Packard's budget ranged from $4,000 to $6,000.

An important, and practical, consideration for companies is not to buy more technology than is needed. The business need should dictate the technology. Based upon the work the employee will be doing, the company should determine the value of the investment to be made on their behalf.

It is usually best if employers provide the equipment for a home office, but many companies require the telecommuter to provide at least some of the equipment.

Another concern for many organizations may be security. This is a concern that can be addressed and, in fact, many large financial institutions manage remote workers — and telecommuters — regularly.

4.1 Office equipment and tools

Generally speaking, an employee working from an off-site location will need access to the same tools and equipment that allow him or her to be effective and productive in the office. Consider, for instance, the needs of a technical writer: He or she would need a computer with word processing software. To communicate with those back at the office, he or she would also need a telephone and email capability.

Depending on the type of work involved and the need for conferencing between clients — internal and external — it may also be necessary to consider conference calling and other special options for the telephone service. A fax machine may not be necessary if the employee can send documents via email. Similarly, a photocopier may not be necessary if the telecommuter has administrative support available through the head office. And, of course, the technical writer will need a desk, office chair, filing space, and office supplies.

When considering the equipment necessary to establish an off-site work space, it is important to achieve a balance between nice-to-have items and their impact on resources and productivity. It might be nice for a technical writer working with colleagues in various locations to have access to teleconferencing equipment, but it might not have enough impact on productivity to justify the expense.

When providing equipment for employees, one important consideration is compatibility with the equipment at the main location. The employee's computer, for instance, should be powerful enough to accommodate the type of work he or she will be doing. Software programs should be the same type and version as coworkers will be using, and email programs should be compatible with those at the head office.

Who should pay for this equipment? For a number of reasons, it is best if the employer covers the costs. If you own the equipment, you have the right to tell the employee to use that equipment for business only. This can be particularly important if the employee will have access to sensitive company or customer information. Owning the equipment will also allow you to make decisions about the type of hardware, software, and other peripherals the employee should be using, and will ensure that your information-system staff are able to provide support for that equipment.

4.2 Safety considerations

There are a variety of safety issues to be considered when setting up a home office, and, of course, there is the issue of who should take responsibility for ensuring the safety of the home office.

In November 1999, the Occupational Safety and Health Administration (OSHA) released an ill-fated advisory indicating that employers would be responsible for the safety of employees when working from their homes. The outcry from employers, employees, and citizens was loud and immediate. The letter was withdrawn on January 5, 2000, but the discussions continued. Labor Secretary Alexis M. Herman began conducting a series of meetings with business, labor, and government leaders to review the needs of the growing telecommuting population, intending to issue a new set of guidelines to ensure telecommuters' safety and health. As of 2009, the issue remains unresolved; OSHA regulations neither explicitly include nor exclude telecommuters from coverage. But even without specific rules from OSHA or other agencies, the vast majority of organizations that allow employees to telecommute do have safety provisions and requirements for their at-home workers.

The Federal Aviation Administration (FAA) requires all home-based employees to complete a checklist (see Checklist 1) to aid in assessing the safety of the requested off-site work location.

Employers need to be responsible for employee safety. The problem is that in an era of virtual work, the bounds of that responsibility are very unclear. If an employee is injured due to an electrical shock because of a frayed cord on the computer in his or her home office, which was supplied by the employer, is the employer at fault? Most reasonable adults would say, "Probably." But is the employer at fault if that same employee slipped and fell on the way to the bathroom while working at home? Most reasonable adults would say, "Probably not."

There are obviously no easy answers. The boundaries between work and home are becoming increasingly blurred. The solution is to develop very clear policies and guidelines regarding safety issues of employees working from home.

5. The Characteristics of a Successful Program

Companies large and small, in rural and urban settings, have learned to manage off-site staff relationships effectively. For many, these relationships are simply part of "how we work." For others, they are generated

Even if an employee works from home, the employer should make sure that the employee's home office meets standard safety requirements.

CHECKLIST 1
TELECOMMUTING SAFETY CHECKLIST

FEDERAL AVIATION ADMINISTRATION
SELF-CERTIFICATION SAFETY CHECKLIST FOR
HOME-BASED TELEWORKERS

Name: _____

Organization/Office: _____

Location: _____

Phone: _____

The following checklist is designed to assess the overall safety of the alternate worksite. Each participant should read and complete the self-certification safety checklist. Upon completion, the checklist should be signed and dated by the participating employee and his/her manager.

The alternate worksite is located at: _____

Describe the designated work area: _____

A. WORKPLACE ENVIRONMENT

1. Are temperature, noise, ventilation, and lighting levels adequate to maintain your normal level of job performance?   Yes ( ) No ( )

2. Are all stairs with four or more steps equipped with handrails?   Yes ( ) No ( )

3. Does the electrical system conform to appropriate local building codes?   Yes ( ) No ( )

4. Are aisles, doorways, and corners free of obstructions to permit visibility and movement?   Yes ( ) No ( )

5. Are file cabinets and storage closets arranged so drawers and doors do not open into walkways?   Yes ( ) No ( )

6. Are chairs free of loose casters (wheels) and are legs of the chairs sturdy?   Yes ( ) No ( )

7. Are the phone lines, electrical cords, and extension wires secured under a desk or alongside a baseboard?   Yes ( ) No ( )

8. Is the office space neat, clear, and free of excessive amounts of combustibles?   Yes ( ) No ( )

9. Are floor surfaces (including carpets) clean, dry, level, and free of worn or frayed seams?   Yes ( ) No ( )

10. Is there enough light for reading?   Yes ( ) No ( )

B. COMPUTER WORKSTATION (IF APPLICABLE)

11. Is your chair adjustable?   Yes ( ) No ( )

12. Is your back adequately supported by a backrest?   Yes ( ) No ( )

13. Is your computer monitor eye-level?   Yes ( ) No ( )

14. When keying, are your forearms close to parallel with the floor?   Yes ( ) No ( )

15. Are your wrists fairly straight when keying?   Yes ( ) No ( )

Employee Signature _____ Date _____

Manager Signature _____ Date _____

Attach a copy of this checklist to your telework agreement, forward to your telework coordinator and retain a copy for your records.

Source: FAA 2006 Telework HROI

through individual requests. Regardless of the way the need arises, success depends on careful planning and well-established guidelines as well as appropriate selection of both the positions and the people who will work in off-site locations.

Decisions about these arrangements should be made for the right reasons. You should not institute a telecommuting program, for instance, simply because an employee has requested the option or because it seems to be a current trend. Like any other business decision you make, the decision to allow employees to work in non-traditional locations should be based on legitimate and demonstrable business benefits.

6. Case Study

Alpine Access is a call center provider with 7,500 employees working from their homes as customer service and tech support reps for companies like J. Crew, Office Depot, EDS, and financial services companies. The company was built around the philosophy that casting a wide net — recruiting employees from across the country, rather than just those who live within commuting distance — would allow for opportunities to attract a more qualified workforce. According to Christopher Carrington, CEO, the philosophy has worked.

"We started as a 100 percent virtual company and we've just started our twelfth year in business," says Carrington. Carrington credits founder Jim Ball with the initial impetus to start the firm after having spent time in a call center environment himself and noting two longstanding problems in the industry — attrition or turnover, and call quality. By drawing staff from a broader geographic area — and by allowing for flexibility in work hours and environment — the firm has overcome both of those challenges.

The average worker at Alpine Access is 41 years old. About 80 percent of the workforce has some form of college education — either

There are many good reasons to implement a telecommuting program, including cost savings, increased productivity, and increased employee recruitment and retention.

a two-year associate degree or a four-year degree. About 10 percent of the workforce has an advanced degree.

"We've come to find that this is a more productive and efficient environment," says Carrington. "The virtual world offers us tools that allow for much greater connectivity," he adds; "All of our calls are being monitored and reported 100 percent of the time. Each of the call center professionals is connected to their supervisor via instant messaging and to their peers via chat rooms. At any point in time if they run into a challenge or have a question they don't know the answer to, they can immediately access anywhere from 50 to 100 helpers to respond to their question."

Carrington adds that just because you have the technology to allow distance work, doesn't mean that distance work will work. "The real secret sauce of this is the underlying business processes that enable you, as a company, to do virtual hiring, virtual training, and the virtual management of these employees," he says. It's not about the technology.

Hiring the right people — as in any work environment — is critical, notes Carrington. "It's quite frankly a very different kind of employee that you'd hire for an at-home job versus a job in a call center," he says. "In a home office environment, you really have to have very self-motivated, very disciplined employees who can get up each morning, make their way to the coffee pot, put on their slippers, and sign in," he says.

"You really need to adjust your profile to the type of person you want to hire."

There are adjustments on the employer side as well, he notes, most of them relating to the need to be more flexible in terms of processes and open to new solutions. For instance, he says, "One of the reasons workers are looking for this kind of environment is for greater life-based flexibility. So, they may not be able to work eight hours straight. Maybe they want to work four in the middle of the day and four in the evening. Maybe they can't work certain days because they need to drive an elderly parent to a doctor's appointment. As an employer, you need to be able to have that flexibility as to when that person can get their time in."

Ultimately, he says, the flexibility pays off. "There's a large, untapped labor force out there that would never go to work in a call center, but for one reason or another had a primary reason to be at home — the business model we have was started under that premise and it's been a great success."

Chapter 3
POLICIES AND PROCEDURES

"It is [company] policy to offer a telecommuting program that will enhance operational efficiency, promote goals, and enrich the quality of work life."

— Department of Transportation
Telecommuting Handbook

Executive Summary

What can I do to control overtime expenses among my off-site staff members?

Hourly or nonexempt employees need to be compensated for hours they work in excess of 40 hours in a work week. This means off-site staff and telecommuters as well. One way of addressing this issue with hourly staff, not unlike dealing with the issue of overtime with traditional staff, is to communicate clearly with off-site or at-home employees that they are expected to work no more than their scheduled time. Any overtime must be pre-approved by the employee's manager, and accurate records of hours worked must be kept.

Could I be charged with discrimination based on a decision to let a certain employee work a flexible schedule or work at home and not another?

Employers may not discriminate in making decisions related to employees based on their race, gender, national origin, age, religion, or with respect to certain disabilities. The need to treat employees equitably also applies to off-site staff and telecommuters and is an important reason why the decision to allow an employee to work in an alternative arrangement must be based on objective criteria. Decisions should not be based solely on the employee's personal/family needs, and employers should never show favoritism toward certain individuals.

Can I be required to allow a disabled employee to telecommute?

The Americans with Disabilities Act (ADA) requires employers to make "reasonable accommodations" for employees with physical or mental disabilities. In some cases, working from home or telecommuting can offer a reasonable accommodation, meeting the needs of both the organization and the disabled worker. While it is likely that courts could require companies that have telecommuting programs to offer telecommuting as an option to disabled workers, it is not likely that courts would require this same accommodation from companies that do not otherwise offer telecommuting as an option.

As there is no national policy regarding disabled Canadians, the possibility of such a requirement is yet more reduced in Canada.

If an employee working at home is injured at home, is he or she eligible for Workers' Compensation?

Employees working from their homes are eligible for workers' compensation benefits if injured during the "course and scope of employment." The issue of whether, and to what extent, employers are liable for the safety of their employees when they are working out of their homes has been the source of much discussion recently. As an employer, you should establish standards for safety and require employees to follow those standards.

Should I require access to an employee's home office?

The ability to visit an employee at his or her home location should be an issue that is addressed in your policies. Visits should be made for business purposes only and should be announced in advance. Issues of employee privacy and company liability surface here, as does concern over potential claims of inappropriate behavior between the visitor and the employee. Can you, as a manager, go to an employee's home to check up on him or her? Yes, but you may not want to. If you do, make sure that you reserve this right and establish some guidelines related to the hours you may visit and the length of notice you should provide.

POLICIES AND PROCEDURES

There are myriad details to consider when establishing relationships or arrangements with employees who will work from off-site locations. It can be the little things that often create the most frustration and require the most effort— things like coming up with an appropriate contract for the program, dealing with performance measurement, or figuring out how to deal with certain legal issues that affect the employee/employer relationship. This chapter discusses the kinds of policies and procedures that you will have to implement in your business to make these arrangements work most effectively. See the Appendixes for sample policies, agreements, and guidelines that have made flexible arrangements, as well as formal telecommuting programs, a success for other organizations.

1. Policy Considerations

In organizations with multiple locations that may require the supervision of employees at various sites, overall organizational policies generally apply, with some exceptions that might be specific to each area's specific characteristics. For instance, one site may have a large fitness facility, while another may have a walking path; one site may have a cafeteria, another may not; access to the building may vary, etc. But, aside from specific physical differences that may require minor variations in policy, the broad organizational policies will apply to all employees, regardless of where they are physically located.

Other types of flexible arrangements — telecommuting programs, for instance — will require specific policies to address the issues related to use of company property, communication requirements, etc.

The more specific and clear you can be about the requirements and processes for your non-traditional work arrangements, the fewer misunderstandings or problems you will encounter. Considering policy and procedure issues before you receive requests from employees will help you make good decisions based upon the needs of your organization.

There are a number of policy issues you will want to consider, many of which are listed below.

1.1 Work hours

One of the benefits that telecommuting employees receive is flexibility in hours of work. But that flexibility must still be tied to the needs of the workplace — including the needs of coworkers and customers (internal and external). Being available to take phone calls or respond to email messages may be critical for some positions, but not others. For example, an employee working in a virtual call center operation and answering calls at home would need to be available to take calls from customers at specific, established times throughout the day. A computer programmer working at home, however, may not have the same access requirements. Each position will vary, but for each position, you should very clearly indicate the hours you expect the employee to be working.

1.2 Work assignments

How will work assignments be provided? Will the employee be required to meet or contact the supervisor on a regularly scheduled basis to discuss assignments, or will assignments be made as they occur? What will the assignments consist of?

1.3 Evaluation

How will the employee's work be evaluated? What level of productivity will be expected? What are the criteria by which the employee's work output will be judged? Be specific. By clearly outlining expectations at the outset, you can avoid misunderstandings and frustration later.

1.4 Salary and benefits

What will the employee's pay be? Will the employee be paid by the hour or have a salary? What benefits will apply?

1.5 Overtime

One of the concerns that many employers have about allowing employees to work from home is that they cannot be monitored. The potential exists for more time to be devoted to a project than might be necessary. One way to address this concern, particularly with hourly employees, is to have a policy that overtime will be not allowed unless approved by the supervisor.

Another is to establish clear expectations about productivity. This is, of course, easier to do when you have a number of employees whose work output can be compared.

1.6 Equipment

Will the employer provide equipment for the employee? Will the employee be allowed to use his or her own equipment? If the employee can use his or her own equipment, will he or she be compensated for that use? Will repairs to employee-owned equipment be paid by the employer? Be specific in outlining your equipment policies, addressing issues such as confidentiality, personal use, upgrades, and return of equipment upon termination.

2. Documenting Your Policies and Procedures

Whether outlined in a specific telecommuting policy, contract, or agreement, or included as part of existing policies and procedures that impact all workers, companies should be certain that they are providing clear and specific written documentation of the understanding between them and any off-site staff. Policies should address all of the details that will impact how the arrangement works, how the employee will interact with the head office, and what the company's expectations are for the relationship. (Note: these expectations will serve as a key part of training for off-site staff, as well as their managers — see Chapter 6.)

2.1 Policy statement

It is very important to take the time to develop a policy specific to your organization's unique needs. While various sample policies are available and may be useful as a starting point, your policy should be customized to the culture and operations of your organization and should provide a summary of your organization's position regarding flexible work arrangements. Key elements that should be included are:

- A statement that the flexible work arrangement is at the employer's discretion and that the employer/manager is responsible for determining when/where work will be performed in accordance with business need.

- Criteria for identifying eligible positions and incumbents (e.g., tenure with the organization, minimum performance level, job types).

- Terms and conditions of the arrangement (e.g., types of flexible options offered, communication requirements, ability to alter arrangement at management's discretion).

- Core hours and a clear system and guidelines for reporting hours worked. In addition, employers should include language indicating that unauthorized work is prohibited and a process/procedure for the approval of overtime hours.

- Any specific communication requirements — e.g., "face time" in the office, conference call or meeting attendance expectations, etc.

- Equipment (e.g., what type will be required, who will purchase — employer or employee, who will support/insure).

- Workers' compensation and safety statement notifying employees that any injuries sustained at home in the course of work need to be reported, as well as an explanation of the mechanism for reporting.

- Confidential information and expectations for its protection from unauthorized observers or use.

- How performance will be evaluated and relevance to continued flexible arrangement.

- The policy should make it clear that the ability to work under a flexible arrangement is not an entitlement or perk, but a business imperative that will be monitored and modified based on business need.

You may wish to specify the supervisor's role in determining the details of these off-site arrangements. For example, you might discuss the supervisor's right to determine the length, duration, and time frames of the arrangement (i.e., how many days per week are appropriate), and/or the supervisor's evaluation schedule and the criteria by which the employee's performance will be judged.

You may also wish to address specific requirements of the program, such as —

- requiring a signed telecommuting work agreement for all participants in a formal telecommuting program, and/or
- requiring training as a prerequisite to working in an off-site capacity.

For employees working from home locations, you might also consider including in your policy statement some discussion of what is not acceptable. For example, you might state that working from home is not a solution for care of dependants.

2.2 Selection criteria

Specific selection criteria will help you avoid discrimination charges arising out of claims of favoritism. Criteria may include such traits as self-motivation, strong communication skills, and the ability to work independently. Selection criteria might also include length-of-service requirements and consideration based on employee evaluations (e.g., an employee may work in an off-site role if he or she has received "satisfactory or higher" ratings on performance evaluations for the past X years). In addition, selection criteria should include factors related to the types of jobs or tasks that can be performed off-site. The more specific you are as to what criteria are acceptable, the more smoothly your program will run.

The Department of Transportation *Telecommuting Handbook* states:

Participants should be employed by (company) for more than 90 days, though special situations could occur that would permit a new employee to telecommute, particularly special need individuals. Employees in a temporary, trainee, or probationary position would not be eligible to telecommute, as these employees usually need close supervision and frequent interaction with supervisors or mentors.

2.3 Expectations/responsibilities of off-site employees

The contract should outline the expectations that the company has of its off-site staff, detailing as much as possible, from furnishings to security issues. The Department of Transportation provides a condensed summary of expectations in its *Telecommuting Handbook*:

All telecommuters will be required to sign and abide by a written letter of agreement, participate in mandatory evaluations, and, for home work situations, provide an adequate home work station that ensures privacy and a lack of interruptions. Telecommuters must be responsible for the security of all official data, protection of government furnished equipment and property, and carrying out the mission of (the company) in an alternate work setting. Performance will be evaluated on finished assignments under a management by results approach. Participating in the Telecommuting Program is offered only with the agreement that it is the employee's responsibility to provide a proper work environment.

2.4 Work schedules

The requirements of each individual position will determine the hours in which the work needs to take place. Certain positions (in-bound telephone sales representatives, for instance) may be required to be available during certain hours of the day, while others (computer programmers, for example) may not have such restrictions. The Department of Transportation *Telecommuting Handbook* provides a very good example of how to approach this issue:

> Work schedules will vary according to the individual arrangement between employee and supervisor. All schedules will be agreed upon, in advance, and should be on a fixed schedule … All regulations regarding absence and leave apply to telecommuters. Supervisors must approve work schedules, in advance, to ensure the employee's time and attendance records are properly certified and to preclude any liability for premium or overtime pay, unless specifically approved, in advance. Compensatory time may be granted in lieu of overtime pay in accordance with applicable regulations. Periodic adjustment to the work schedule is desirable to achieve the best mix of organizational requirements and employee performance.

2.5 Equipment and supplies

This section of the agreement should outline, in detail, the equipment and supplies that will be provided by the company and those that will be the responsibility of the off-site employee. Standards, where applicable, should also be included (i.e., requirements for certain types of furniture based on safety considerations, etc.). Indicate, also, whether and to what extent the employee will be responsible for maintenance and repair of equipment, what the employer's role will be, and how repairs will be handled (i.e., equipment will need to be brought into the office or the company will send a repair person to the employee's home location). Again, be as specific as possible to avoid any employee confusion or dissatisfaction. The Department of Transportation *Telecommuting Handbook* discusses this matter in detail: Supervisors may authorize use of computers and other telecommunications equipment in a home office, provided the equipment is used only for official business and requested equipment is available for use in a home office. Participation in a telecommuting agreement may be contingent on the availability of equipment or the availability of funds to purchase equipment needed to perform the official duties. Each arrangement must be examined on a case-by-case basis before final approval in order to make decisions on the type of equipment needed and its availability.

The employee must protect all equipment from possible theft and environmental damage. In cases of damage to unsecured equipment by non-employees, the employee may be held liable for repair or replacement of the equipment, software, etc., in compliance with applicable regulations on negligence. The employee must notify the supervisor immediately following a malfunction of (company-owned) equipment. If repairs are extensive, the employee may be asked to report to the traditional office until repairs are completed.

2.6 Insurance

You should verify what type of coverage is afforded the off-site employee based upon your existing insurance policy, and decide whether the employee will be responsible for providing any additional coverage. The employee should indemnify the company from any injuries claimed by any third parties and should be required to maintain appropriate insurance coverage for these types of claims.

2.7 Employer's right to inspect workplace

Clearly indicate if and when the company or manager will have the right to inspect or visit the employee's off-site work location. For instance, you may want to reserve the right to access the home office for purposes of safety inspections, accident investigations, equipment audits, or other business-related matters. Visits are usually based upon reasonable notice — generally 24 hours, or less, if agreed to by the employee.

2.8 Privacy and confidentiality

Employees working from their homes, particularly those who are connected to the home office electronically, present a certain amount of security risk for your organization. Consider having these employees sign confidentiality agreements. Indicate in the agreement whether or not the employee may use computer equipment for non-work-related activities. Security procedures must be discussed in detail, with emphasis upon the need for strict adherence to the procedures.

2.9 Performance measurement

Off-site employees and their managers should work together to come up with applicable quantitative measures of performance. These measures should be documented as part of the agreement and should clearly indicate what the expectations are of the employee in terms of quantity and quality of work, as well as how often and in what manner the employee's performance will be measured.

2.10 Company policies

If a separate policy is being created to address an off-site employee's unique situation, or as part of a formal telecommuting program, include a statement in the policy document to indicate that these employees will also be required to abide by all other existing company policies and procedures, except as they differ from specific items as outlined in the agreement.

2.11 Termination of the agreement

As "exit strategy" should be outlined at the onset of any special agreement allowing an employee to work in an off-site setting or establishing a telecommuting arrangement. The agreement should include a section dealing with the potential termination of the agreement by the company, manager, or employee. It should detail the situation(s) under which the agreement might be terminated (i.e., inability to perform work duties as outlined in the agreement). It should also discuss the employee's options upon termination of the agreement — can the employee maintain the position in-house, can he or she apply for another in-house position, or is the employee terminated from the company? The termination agreement must also address the disposition of any company equipment that has been purchased for the employee's use at home.

2.12 Employment-at-will disclaimer

A telecommuting or alternative work arrangement agreement does not constitute a contract of employment. The agreement should indicate, as applicable, that the employee remains employed on an at-will basis and can be terminated with or without cause and with or without notice.

3. Case Study

Aflac is the number one provider of guaranteed-renewable insurance in the United States. The company was founded in 1955 by three brothers, who started the company in six small rented rooms in Columbus, Georgia. Aflac's insurance products provide protection to more than 40 million people worldwide. Women comprise nearly 70 percent of the company's employee population, about 50 percent of management (supervisory level and beyond), and about 30 percent of senior executives (VP level and beyond). Compressed work weeks, flextime, and telecommuting arrangements are valuable options that make a real difference to employees.

Aflac's commitment to its employees goes beyond lip service. From its earliest beginning, the founding brothers recognized the critical role that satisfied employees would play in ensuring satisfied policyholders and it would seem that no holes have been barred as the company seeks to attract and retain committed, talented, and loyal employees. According to company lore, the brothers who founded Aflac often said: "If you take care of the employees, they'll take care of the business," a philosophy that is still embraced today. One of Aflac's guiding principles is to: "Provide an enriching and rewarding workplace for our employees."

Its efforts have been widely recognized. Aflac has been included in *Fortune* magazine's listing of "100 Best Companies to Work for" for ten consecutive years and was recognized in 2006 as a *Working Mother* "100 Best" company, celebrated for creating a work environment that is especially hospitable to all women, including working mothers. In making family-friendly policies — including flextime, child care, and telecommuting — the norm, Aflac continues to create a corporate culture that encourages the retention and promotion of its female employees.

While responding to the needs of employees provides benefit and is widely lauded by Aflac employees, Aflac believes these efforts serve important business needs and, because of this, has continued to explore and expand its flexible work offerings as demands shift and change.

Aflac employees enjoy a supportive work environment with an open-door management philosophy, excellent benefits, competitive salaries — and significant flexibility. The company provides a variety of flexible work options including varying shifts, such as 6:00 a.m. to 2:30 p.m., 8:00 a.m. to 5:00 p.m., or 3:00 p.m. to 11:00 p.m., and a weekend schedule of 12 hours per day Thursday through Saturday. Aflac also has a telework program that allows some employees to work from home.

While the variety of shifts is designed to meet the family needs of workers, flexibility must also serve the business. Compressed work week options have been in place for about seven years. Alternate schedules are more recent and have been in place for about two years. Requests for scheduling variation are processed through supervisors, yet efforts are made to support what is an employee-driven system where workers have control for choosing their schedules. Feedback from employees about needs, preferences and ideas for new innovation are gathered through focus groups and other sources.

In addition to enjoying flexibility in scheduling, employees are encouraged to maintain a healthy work/life balance and are supported in those efforts through a generous Personal Time Off (PTO) policy that allows them to attend family activities and events — or to attend to their own personal needs.

Chapter 4
OFF-SITE RELATIONSHIPS
WITH EXISTING STAFF

"[Telecommuting] is not a right, it's a management alternative."

— Alan Coleman of Sprint

Executive Summary

What if all of my employees decide they want to work off-site?

It's unlikely that all of your employees will decide that working off-site or in telecommuting arrangements is right for them. In fact, many employees prefer to work in the traditional setting. Remember, whether an off-site job assignment is appropriate for an individual or a position is a decision that must be made by the manager and the organization. Of course, there are a growing number of organizations that operate entirely virtually — with no single, physical location.

Is working in an off-site setting appropriate for hourly workers?

In general, yes. However, you will want to check the employment law statutes in your area to make sure there are no laws that prohibit non-exempt employees from working as telecommuters.

Can managers work in off-site settings or as telecommuters?

Yes! In fact, many managers do operate, in effect, as remote managers when they are responsible for supervising employees who may be located in other offices — even in other countries!

What are the characteristics of a successful off-site employee?

Good employees make good employees, whether physically located in a central location or working out of their home. Those who will thrive in off-site assignments are independent thinkers, self-starters, and productive workers who clearly understand the requirements of the job and can work effectively with little or no supervision.

How do I deal with employees who wish to, but are not able to work in a remote or off-site setting?

Working in an alternative location should be explained to employees as a job variation rather than a benefit. Your policies should clearly indicate the types of positions and personal qualifications that are required for employees eligible to work in these arrangements. Beyond this, there may be other flexible work options that employees not right for off-site arrangements can take advantage of — e.g., flexible scheduling or job sharing.

Does an employee have the right to work off-site or telecommute?

No. The decision on whether or not to allow an employee a flexible work arrangement should be made by the employer based on the appropriateness of both the position and the employee's skills and capabilities. This decision should be based upon specific criteria that are applied to all potential candidates.

OFF-SITE RELATIONSHIPS WITH EXISTING STAFF

Now that you have a good idea of what is involved in managing off-site staff and the elements of a formal telecommuting program, it is time to think about the people who will ultimately make the program a success. It is time to think about the employees!

In the vast majority of situations, employees who work in off-site locations come from within the organization and have held a position with the company for some time before making the transition. There are obvious benefits to selecting employees to work in off-site arrangements from your existing staff. You already know these people! You've had a chance to view their work habits and performance. You know which of your employees are independent and proactive and which employees need constant supervision and direction.

But there can be downfalls as well, particularly if you don't take the time to make informed and carefully considered choices about which employees are offered these opportunities. Even when assigning employees to branch locations or other affiliated sites where they won't have direct supervision, it is important to consider the traits and characteristics of these employees to ensure that they're right for this type of "remote" work.

Just as you need a system for creating policies and procedures for those situations where employees are working in a nontraditional location, so too do you need a systematic approach to considering individual candidates. How structured your selection criteria are will depend on your company's culture as well as on your comfort level with the concept of managing off-site staff. Even companies that have been committed to these flexible arrangements for some time often have very stringent criteria for selecting candidates.

Alan Coleman of Sprint, a company that has been practicing telecommuting for years — "since modems were created," Coleman says — has established what he refers to as "a fairly laborious process to becoming a telecommuter." Sprint has 650 full-time telecommuters with more than 20,000 employees telecommuting informally, according to Coleman.

The process was formalized, he says, for a number of reasons:

(a) To ensure that people wouldn't begin pouring home in massive numbers

(b) To make sure that management had adequate knowledge of the job functions that were being performed at home

(c) To allow executives to see how business units were actually managing their individual units

(d) To allow for accurate evaluation of the success, failure, and costs of telecommuting to the company

At Sprint, the managers drive the process of telecommuting. That's not to say that individual employees can't request that their position be considered for telecommuting. It simply means that the manager is in charge and is expected to make an appropriate determination of whether telecommuting is or is not appropriate for his or her particular work unit — and a particular employee.

1. Working Remotely Is Not for Everyone

Just as some jobs are more appropriate for off-site arrangements than others, certain employees are more suited to working in these situations than other employees. Some employees may not even be interested. You may be surprised to find, in fact, that a number of your staff actually prefer the camaraderie and sense of team that the workplace holds. Other employees may simply realize that they are not self-motivated enough to be productive away from the traditional workplace. Still others have home situations that might make it inconvenient or untenable for them to work there. And many people will find it difficult to maintain a division between home-life and work-life when home and work share a location.

2. Selection Criteria

Some of the criteria for selecting employees who will be good telecommuters are admittedly subjective. Susan Thomas, who leads a telecommuting program for CIGNA, an employee benefits company, says, "We're looking for people who are independent workers, meaning they're comfortable with working alone physically, they're self-motivated, they are good communicators in terms of letting people know where they are, asking questions when questions need to be asked, and seeking out resources." CIGNA has had a formal corporate policy on telecommuting since 1991 and had at least 1,000 active telecommuters in 2000 — many who are responsible for claims processing, but also professional workers including nursing staff and training professionals. Typically, employees work for the company prior to becoming telecommuters, but some positions — in the virtual sales offices, for instance — hire people as telecommuters. In addition to the soft skills, CIGNA also looks at some quantifiable characteristics. Most telecommuters are required to have six months of service with the company; they must also perform at a level that meets standards, and they must be proficient with a computer.

Successful telecommuters —

- *Stay connected with coworkers and the boss.* This requires a certain amount of proactive communication. Rather than waiting for the phone to ring or for the email message to arrive, successful off-site employees take the initiative to stay connected.

- *Are well organized.* Many employees who move from the traditional work setting to an off-site location, particularly a home location, come from environments in which they had ready access to administrative staff. When working alone, that access may be limited — or nonexistent.

- *Get out of the house.* Working off-site doesn't mean burrowing. Successful remote employees take advantage of opportunities to network with coworkers, peers, and other colleagues by making lunch dates, being active in professional associations, and generally staying in touch.

- *Separate home from work.* When working from home, it can be difficult to avoid the lure of personal tasks — like washing clothes or taking care of children and pets. It's important to learn how to establish clear boundaries between home and work.

- *Make technology their friend.* Technology has made working from remote locations in virtually any setting possible and popular. The many tools like email, group scheduling, and teleconferencing make it easy to stay connected, regardless of physical and geographic barriers.

- *Know when to take a break.* A common downfall of working outside the traditional work environment, according to those who have experienced it, is the tendency to work too much!

Certain employees may prove to be ill-suited to working in an environment where they have no direct supervision and, potentially, limited contact with others. They may include —

- employees who have a high need for social interaction,

- employees who are easily distracted by outside demands and interruptions,

- employees who need the office setting to provide an environment conducive to work, and

- employees who do not have adequate child-care arrangements or supportive family situations.

Working in nontraditional environments — or at remote locations — is not an option that should be available to all employees. Your decision on whether to place an employee in a branch or remote location, or to allow that employee to work from home in a telecommuting arrangement will depend upon the demands and characteristics of the job as well as the personal traits of the employee. Selection criteria should be carefully considered and clearly outlined in your policies and contract, as appropriate.

3. Assessing Candidates

How can you determine whether employees will be suited to this type of work? Your own observation of their performance during their employment with your company can certainly provide some indications. In addition, you will want to spend some time speaking with the employee and exploring the pros and cons of alternative work arrangements to provide both of you with a sense of whether or not these options will be appropriate.

At Merrill Lynch, employees and their managers worked jointly to develop telecommuting arrangements, according to Janice Miholics, vice president, manager of private client technology for alternative work arrangements. The first step for employees interested in telecommuting is to submit a telecommuting proposal. The proposal outlines the days of the week — and even hours of the day — during which the employee would like to telecommute. In addition, the employee is asked to include information on why he or she would be a good candidate for telecommuting, what the benefits are to the employee, to the manager, and to their clients. It is then up to the manager to review the proposal and approve or deny the request. Janice's group reviews all proposals, both approved and denied. This provides a good checkpoint, allowing, for instance, the opportunity to review any rejections and ensure that there are no underlying employee-relations issues. Managers are also expected to document reasons that a candidate was not selected and to spend time with the employee to indicate what the employee may need to do in order to be considered at some future date.

Using an assessment tool in the selection of telecommuting candidates is an effective way to avoid any charges of arbitrariness. Such a tool can provide both the employee and his or her manager with an indication of readiness or appropriateness for telecommuting.

ALLearnatives®, a company in Wexford, Pennsylvania that provides learning resources and consulting services to individuals and organizations involved in telecommuting, offers the following self-assessment for those interested in telecommuting. This tool can serve as a good starting point in discussions between managers and employees on their readiness or suitability for a telecommuting position.

TABLE 4
ASSESSMENT FOR SUITABILITY FOR TELECOMMUTING

True	False	I believe I:
		Enjoy working independently.
		Like to think through and resolve problems myself.
		Am a high-initiative person.
		Am not a procrastinator.
		Can set and stick to a schedule.
		Like to organize and plan.
		Am a self-disciplined person.
		Am able and willing to handle administrative tasks.

TABLE 4 continued

		Can balance attention to major objectives and small details.
		Do not need constant interaction with people.
		Can work effectively with little or no feedback from others.
		Enjoy being in my own home.
		Do not need frequent feedback or coaching.
		Have the required level of verbal and written communication skills.
		Can pace myself to avoid both overworking and wasting time.
		Can resist a refrigerator that is only a few steps away.

JOB APPROPRIATENESS — My job:

		Requires minimal face-to-face interaction.
		Involves many responsibilities that can be met by phone, fax, or modem.
		Entails accountabilities that can be quantified, measured, and monitored.
		Affords me the freedom to manage my work as I see best.
		Does not require frequent interaction with work associates.
		Involves coworkers who are supportive and collaborative.

HOME OFFICE SPACE/EQUIPMENT — I have a space in my home office that:

		Has an adequate amount of work space for my current needs.
		Would provide opportunities for future expansion.
		Has an adequate amount of storage space.
		Has adequate lighting.
		Has sufficient ventilation.
		Has a safe number of electrical circuits.
		Is quiet enough to allow me to concentrate.
		Provides appropriate separation from home/family distractions.
		Is a pleasant and comfortable space I'd enjoy working in.
		Is a reasonable distance from needed business services.
		Has no zoning or lease restrictions that preclude telecommuting.
		Has adequate insurance coverage to protect business equipment.

FAMILY SUPPORT — My family:

		Is supportive of my desire to telecommute and will react positively.
		Is willing to help me to minimize distractions and interruptions.
		Will not require care or involvement from me during work hours.
		Can accept my need to focus on work during business hours.
		Is stable and has no relationship conflicts that would be distracting.

When reviewing the form with potential telecommuting candidates, give special consideration to those items that the potential telecommuter has marked as "false." These are the areas that represent potential barriers to success.

Note that the criteria go beyond personal characteristics like "enjoy working independently" to take into account considerations related to the job itself, the home-office environment, and even the family. Each of these characteristics can have an impact on the telecommuter's success, and each needs to be carefully considered.

4. Traits of Successful Teleworkers

A successful employee is a successful employee, whether he or she works from home, at a branch location, or at the head office. Assuming that the job is appropriate for off-site work, you probably already have a good idea of how your employee will perform. Yet there are some specific skills that require particular emphasis in off-site positions.

Sample 1 is a useful summary of the traits found to be common among successful telecommuters, drawn from the ALLearnatives® assessment tool.

Alongside these core requirements, you will want to look for other qualifications that will make the transition to off-site or non-traditional work that much more smooth for your employees and, ultimately, for your business.

5. Perils and Pitfalls

Your company and management staff should be aware of some common issues that may arise when selecting staff for off-site work, or approving such requests.

5.1 It just doesn't work

One of the greatest potential pitfalls involved in selecting employees to work remotely or in off-site locations is choosing the wrong employee. Fortunately, it's a pitfall that can be overcome. Not all employees will thrive in these roles, regardless of how careful the selection process was, how thoroughly the employee was trained and prepared, and how exceptional the support from the workplace is. Sometimes it just doesn't work out. That's okay. In your policy or contract, recognize the possibility of failure and clearly indicate what happens when the situation does not prove to be successful. Address such issues as —

COMMON TRAITS OF SUCCESSFUL TELECOMMUTERS

ALLearnatives®

Enjoy working independently. An employee who is able to tackle assignments without a great deal of intervention from his or her manager and who feels comfortable working alone, without frequent interaction with coworkers, would be more comfortable working as a telecommuter than an employee who thrives in a team environment.

Like to think through and resolve problems on their own. An employee who asks frequent questions and needs constant reassurance about his or her progress may have a difficult time working in an unsupervised environment. At a minimum, this employee would need to have some well-established communication channels available to maintain ties to the workplace.

Demonstrate high initiative. Employees who thrive in telecommuting settings have demonstrated their independence through a high level of initiative on the job. They are the employees who don't wait to be told what to do next — they generate ideas, tackle assignments, and are able to remain productive with little outside reinforcement.

Do not procrastinate. Production is the name of the game in any employee/employer relationship, and telecommuting is certainly no exception. The issue of procrastination goes directly to many managers' concerns about the "out of sight, out of mind" conundrum. Employees who consistently meet deadlines (without having to frantically pull things together at the last minute) will be best suited for telecommuting. Employees who frequently fail to get assignments completed on time and need a great deal of prompting to move forward would probably not be good telecommuting candidates.

Can set and stick to a schedule. Since employees working from their homes are not directly observed or managed, they need to be comfortable and adept at setting and sticking to their own work schedules. Many organizations require that employees indicate specific times that they will be "working," and this is a good practice. Yet, beyond this, telecommuters must also be able to push themselves to be productive when they're away from the formal drivers that they've been used to.

Are able and willing to handle administrative tasks. In the workplace telecommuters may have been able to take advantage of administrative help that may not be available (or may not be as readily available) once they are telecommuting. Will the telecommuter feel comfortable doing his or her own administrative tasks — filing, making photocopies, etc.?

Do not need constant interaction. This can be a difficult point to assess. Even the most gregarious person may feel perfectly at ease working from home. It's an issue that only the individual can truly address. To help in this assessment, you may want to consider the use of a personality inventory such as the Myers-Briggs assessment.

Have the required level of communication skills. Communication is a critical skill for telecommuters. They must recognize the need for, feel comfortable with, and be committed to communicating regularly with people back at the office. They must be able to do this effectively both in written form (email and other written documents) and verbally (telephone, teleconference, regularly scheduled meetings).

Can pace themselves to avoid both overworking and wasting time. Perhaps surprisingly, one of the common problems experienced by telecommuters is working too much. When work is always just a few steps away, it can be difficult not to succumb to the lure of doing just one more thing. Successful telecommuters are able to differentiate between work time and home time.

Reprinted with permission from *101 Tips for Telecommuters* [Copyright©1999] by Debra A. Dinnocenzo.

- How long will the trial period be?

- What criteria will be used to determine the success of the arrangement?

- Will the employee be able to terminate the arrangement? Under what circumstances?

- Will the employee's manager be able to terminate the arrangement? Under what circumstances?

- Will the employee be able to return to his or her traditional position? In what instances might this not be possible?

Both manager and employee should thoroughly review the potential for the arrangement to prove unacceptable before the alternative work assignment begins.

At CIGNA, Susan Thomas says, each telecommuter has an agreement that lists provisions for an unsuccessful off-site situation. "We reserve the right to amend, modify, or terminate the arrangement at any time," she says. "People know what they're getting into."

5.2 It's not fair!

The ability to work from home is frequently viewed as a benefit by employees — particularly by those who do not have this option. This is a very real issue and one that should be considered and addressed.

Having clearly established criteria and a well-defined process for the selection of off-site employees can help prevent problems related to perceived inequities or favoritism. At Sprint, the employee's manager makes the decision of whether or not an employee is able to work away from the main office. "It's made very clear that this is not a right," Alan Coleman says, "it's a management alternative."

Susan Thomas agrees that these issues can be successfully addressed through clearly defined selection criteria and a well-communicated process. "It's like any other decision," she points out. "An analogy might be if you have three people in a department who apply for a specific job — one gets it and the other two don't. As long as you have a concrete reason why, there shouldn't be a problem. The employees may be disappointed, but at least they'll understand."

5.3 My manager won't let me!

Managers need to be receptive to the concept of telecommuting. Problems can develop if one manager allows his or her employees to telecommute and a manager with similar types of employees doesn't. Alan Coleman admits that this can be a problem, even for a company like Sprint, which has embraced the concept of telecommuting and has been practicing telecommuting for quite some time. "One of the biggest challenges companies face is that the corporate mindset today still has visual supervision built in — getting over that is difficult. As people become more reliant on technology, that will fade, but right now, it's still prevailing."

What does he do to address this issue? Nobody at Sprint is forced to participate in telecommuting, but the development of extensive guides and assessments is encouraging. The other key, he says, is that "it absolutely requires top, executive-level support for the culture to shift. It has to be communicated through the entire organization."

6. Case Study

Bob Glantz heads the research team at Access Communications, the nation's fifth-largest independent technology public relations firm. Access has had a very successful telecommuting program in place for years, says Glantz. The program allows account staffers who have reached certain benchmarks to telecommute one day a week. "We provide all the gear, including a broadband connection," says Glantz.

A $14.2 million agency, with 70 full-time employees in San Francisco and New York, the average annual turnover is approximately 15 percent — compared to an industry average of around 34 percent.

Glantz himself telecommutes from his home office in Berkeley, about 11 miles from corporate headquarters in San Francisco and has been doing so for 10 years. "I go into the San Francisco office maybe once a month for staff and management meetings," says Glantz.

The nature of the PR business lends itself to telecommuting, acknowledges Glantz. "If we were a manufacturing firm, telecommuting would be an option for fewer of our staff members," he says. "But, as an information-based business, telecommuting has served us very well over the years."

The essential element in a successful telecommuting relationship, says Glantz, is trust. "You just absolutely have to have trust in the people with whom you're working." And, he adds, people selected for these off-site sorts of relationships need to be vetted very carefully. "It's all about choosing the right people, maintaining the lines of communication, and trusting them to get the job done," he says. "It may not sound like very profound advice, but it's worked well for me over the years."

Chapter 5
RECRUITING EMPLOYEES FOR TELECOMMUTING POSITIONS

"We're at a point in time where we're seeing a fundamental change in the way that work gets done in the world."

— Rick Davis, CEO of online job marketplace Ants.com

Executive Summary

Do off-site staff always come from existing staff?

Not always. While the majority of companies that offer these flexible options do hire from within, there are a growing number of examples of companies that are actually recruiting individuals to serve as telecommuters or to work in virtual organizations. One of the key benefits of recruiting individuals to work in these alternative arrangements is that they can literally be located anywhere. This enlarges the labor pool for employers which can be particularly useful for employers recruiting for highly specialized and hard-to-fill positions.

How can I effectively recruit employees from diverse geographic locations?

The Internet has opened up a wealth of opportunities for employers when recruiting staff of almost any kind. There are a number of recruitment sites online that offer employers, at minimal or no cost, the opportunity to promote open positions and/or to review résumés that have been posted by job seekers. Your own website can also be a good way to promote open positions. In addition, the explosion of social media has provided new opportunities to develop contacts and relationships through connections gained through sites such as LinkedIn and Twitter.

Isn't it risky to hire people sight unseen?

Not necessarily. Consider that some professions have been doing this for decades; freelance writers, for instance, are frequently hired to write for publications, and may never actually meet the editors with whom they are working. The key is to focus on the requirements of the position and to look for evidence that the candidate can meet those requirements (just as when hiring for any traditional position). Also, just because you are hiring for a remote or off-site position doesn't mean that you shouldn't ask the candidates to come to your office for in-person interviews.

What if I make the wrong choice?

What if you make the wrong choice in any hiring situation? Not every candidate will work out and, when this happens, you would follow the steps you would normally follow in terminating any employee.

Is it more important to check the references of candidates for telecommuting positions?

No, but it is equally important. Reference checking is a critical step in any recruitment process. Make sure that you take the time to thoroughly review any applicant's background by contacting past employers and, where possible, speaking with others who may have experience and insight related to the applicant's ability to perform the job.

RECRUITING EMPLOYEES FOR TELECOMMUTING POSITIONS

Most organizations that use telecommuters select them from their existing workforce. Face it: That's the least risky thing to do. You are familiar with these people. They've proven their worth, their commitment, and their efficiency. But what if you really don't have anybody on staff that you feel would be suitable for the position? Worse, what if you're looking for certain skills or experience that just don't seem to exist in your geographic area? Or, as seems to be the case more often these days, what if your organization isn't a brick-and-mortar facility and you don't really care where your employees live, just as long as they can do the job?

Gil Gordon, a widely recognized expert on telecommuting, says that while the "reality today is that the majority of companies select telecommuters from their current workforce, I think that's beginning to change slowly. The nature of the employment relationship is changing overall, with a shift to more use of contractors and consultants and the advent of the so-called virtual organization. It's no longer assumed that the worker needs to be on-site full-time."

One of the real benefits of hiring individuals as telecommuters is that they don't have to live anywhere near your business. Your hiring pool is infinitely large. But the sheer size of this pool can also present a disadvantage when it comes to recruiting. Where do you begin?

Online recruiting is growing exponentially. Finding employees online allows an employer to reach a much broader audience.

The traditional recruitment option — placing a classified ad in your local newspaper — may limit your search unnecessarily. Networking may be equally limited, depending on the geographic scope and background of the people you know. Job fairs may or may not work. In short, the traditional means that have worked for other positions may not work as well when you're recruiting individuals for telecommuting positions.

Fortunately, the realm of recruiting is changing rapidly with the advent of the Internet and social media.

Social media and social networking are "all the rage" these days, of course. But, beyond the purely "social" aspects of sites like Twitter, Facebook, and LinkedIn, does social media represent any legitimate business value? In the area of recruitment, it seems, it definitely does.

1. Social Media for Recruitment

As far back as November 2006, National Public Radio had a spot on its "morning edition" about social networking — http://www.npr.org/templates/story/story.php?storyId=6522523 — and its benefits from a recruiting standpoint. Today, these sites are becoming increasingly relied upon by HR departments as a source of job candidates. In fact, three-quarters of hiring managers check LinkedIn to research the credentials of job candidates, according to a Jump Start Social Media (www.jumpstartsocialmedia.com) poll on how social media is being used in the hiring process. Of the hiring managers surveyed, 75 percent use LinkedIn, 48 percent use Facebook, and 26 percent use Twitter to research candidates before making a job offer. When sourcing job candidates, 66 percent of hiring managers visit LinkedIn, 23 percent visit Facebook and 16 percent use Twitter to find job candidates to fill openings.

Raquel Garcia, an HR consultant, founder and president of Silicon Valley Human Resources (http://siliconvalleyhr.com), says that social media offers a number of benefits for recruitment. First, she says: "you can learn a lot about your potential recruit from their social media pages and find great passive talent online." She has used social media both to source passive job seekers and to check candidates' profiles. She also posts positions she's recruiting for on Facebook and LinkedIn and says she gets "great responses/recommendations."

Jobvite (www.jobvite.com), a San Francisco-based provider of next-generation recruitment solutions, recently published the results of its second annual "Social Recruitment Survey," which found that employers are more satisfied with the quality of candidates from employee referrals and social networks than those from job boards. As a result, companies intend to invest more in these cost-effective candidate sources in 2009, rather than job boards and other traditional sources, including search firms, according to the survey. The viral nature of social media is a key benefit. Those reading the messages may not be looking for a job themselves, but may have a friend or a family member who is.

Because of the "low cost of entry," there are no out-of-pocket costs associated with social media recruitment efforts. Time is money, of course. Some of the "fear" surrounding the use of social media is the time that may be required — or diverted — to learn about and "play with" these tools. Consequently, those considering this option should develop a strategy for their activities to avoid being overcome by the overwhelming amount of information and options available through these sites.

Lauryn Franzoni is executive director of ExecuNet (www.execunet.com), an executive business network, and frequently speaks to HR groups on the strengths and weaknesses of social media recruitment strategies.

The first step in using social networks to find staff, says Franzoni, is determining "what you really want to get out of it." She notes that there are "big, broad social networks out there — and there are also niche networks that support participating types of talent and various expertise." And, she notes, there are also company-specific networks.

"If I'm a hiring manager, I have to figure out what kind of staffing we need, what the characteristics are of the staffing we're going to need, and how those characteristics match up to social networks." Franzoni says that she has found that companies tend to either be focused on entry-level staffing, in which case the broad social networks can be useful — or more skilled positions, where niche networks can be most helpful. It is these skilled positions that most often lend themselves to telecommuting solutions due to the scarcity of candidates. Social media is an excellent way to connect with individuals who are technology savvy a trait that successful telecommuters will certainly need.

Even if you're not currently recruiting or not currently sure that social media holds value for you in terms of recruitment, it doesn't hurt to start "dabbling" in the social media environment.

Before posting an online ad, research the site to make sure it matches the position you're advertising. For example, don't try to find a computer programmer on a job site devoted to telemarketers.

Social media can be used in three primary ways when recruiting:

1. Posting available jobs

2. "Trolling" for potential candidates

3. "Checking out" applicants/interviewees

The Internet makes it easy to find information about applicants to augment the traditional reference-checking process. Sites like LinkedIn provide an opportunity to see what others may have said about the candidate in "recommendations." But, while the ability to learn about candidates by looking at online networking sites can be helpful, Franzoni recommends caution. "You may miss some very good candidates depending on whether you've been able to assess them on something relevant to the job, or you're rating them on personal characteristics," she says.

"As much as we and many other counsel people need to be careful about what they have on their profiles, it's proving to provide a lot more ammunition for hiring managers to rule people out — and they may actually be missing some very good candidates."

Another caution, says Franzoni, is making sure that applicants are being "evaluated based on something relevant to the job, and not on personal characteristics." This is important in terms of ensuring fair hiring practices that do not run afoul of EEOC guidelines.

2. The Internet as a Recruiting Tool

In addition to social media, numerous online recruitment sites are also available. While declining in usage somewhat because of the benefits of sites like LinkedIn and Twitter, these recruitment sites still remain an excellent source of candidates. Some of the more popular sites include Monster Board (www.monster.com), Nation Job (www.nationjob.com), and Career Builder (www.careerbuilder.com). There are hundreds of others.

While the large job boards like Monster Board appeal to the masses, there are a number of industry-specific sites that can help you narrow your search. Sites such as www.showbizjobs.com and www.salesengineer.com provide both employers and job seekers with the ability to target their searches.

Obviously, not all of the online job seekers are looking for telecommuting opportunities. Still, the Internet has been a definite boost both for telecommuters looking for work and for the employers who are looking for them.

The best way to become familiar with the recruiting resources available on the Internet is to review the various services yourself, keeping in mind that you want to find one that is most advantageous for you. Smaller, more specialized services may be more appropriate for your needs, depending on the type of position you are attempting to fill. Just as when you are recruiting through more traditional means, using a combination of resources can be the best way to promote your telecommuting job openings.

There are countless online recruiting sites — with more being developed on a virtually daily basis! Some are devoted specifically to job searches. A quick and easy way to find out information about the latest online job sites is to conduct a search using one of the many online search engines.

VirtualVocations (www.virtualvocations.com) was started in February of 2007 with the sole purpose of providing legitimate and diverse telecommuting employment positions to those interested in working from home. The site has grown rapidly in a short period of time. The site owners wanted to create a site that would offer a wide variety of legitimate virtual positions for those interested in working from home that were not "start-your-own-business" or commission-based types of positions.

Many of the jobs posted are in the technology realm, but positions also appear for salespeople, consultants, writers, designers, etc. Even specialized positions for various types of professionals are included. See Sample 2 for examples of job postings.

1.2 Effective online recruiting

If you're recruiting online, you need to have the same familiarity with these services as you would with any technical or professional journal in which you were advertising. Who are the users of the site? What are their characteristics? How frequently is the site accessed? How widely do they advertise? Is the profession for which you are recruiting well represented?

The use of key words — the search words that online job seekers will enter to pull up your listing — is a critical and often overlooked skill. You need to tie the appropriate keywords to your ads and you need to probe to make sure that your ads are being properly coded. If you have posted ads and wonder why you are not receiving any inquiries, the coding process may be the culprit. Each search engine is different, and you need to take the time to learn how each one functions and what sort of patterns there are in putting the key words together. You

Work-at-Home Accountant

Position is available for a part time Accountant to work on a contract or per project basis. Duration of work is estimated from 4–6+ weeks. Requirements: must have solid accounting background in bank reconciliations; must have 3 years' experience in accounting and references; must be able to work at home with computer and high-speed Internet connection.

Telecommute iPhone Developer

Consulting Group is seeking an experienced iPhone Developer to work on clients' applications. This is an Independent Contractor position and work will involve a variety of projects, including medical applications and games. Potential for full time work after trial period. Must reside in the US. Please submit résumé and hourly rates.

Home-Based Professional Editor/Proofreader

Position is available for a professional editor/proofreader to work from home. Must hold a BS Degree in life sciences or at least 2 years' experience in science-related field. At least 2 years of professional editing experience and experience with AP style guidelines required. Must pay close attention to detail and be available every Wednesday night for 2–4 hours of professional development.

Being very specific in your online job posting will help you eliminate as many undesirable applicants as possible before moving on to the interviewing process.

don't want to code too restrictively or too broadly. Knowledge of how terminology is used in the field from which you're recruiting is a must.

A good way to become familiar with the technology is to practice with your own résumé or advertisement. This will give you insight into how easy or difficult it is to access the online résumés of qualified candidates — or how easy it is for candidates to find your ad. If you post your résumé or ad to a service and it is not pulled up when you enter the key words that you feel are most relevant, something is wrong.

There are literally thousands of individuals searching online job sites for positions. While a very general posting may provide you with countless leads, the more specific you can be, the more clearly you can narrow the market to only those candidates who are uniquely qualified to fill the positions you have available.

1.3 Using your own website

Another rich source of applicants for many organizations is their own website. If you have a website already, consider adding a section detailing your vacant positions. Make your website user-friendly by offering job seekers the ability to search by keywords, location, job title, or pay. Include the option to apply for positions or submit résumés online. Again, being specific and detailed is important. Consider these listings your one opportunity to attract the attention of interested applicants.

Of course, simply including job listings on your site isn't enough to generate response. You need to make sure that potential job seekers know that this information is available. That means promoting your site. Promote your website through traditional communication channels by ensuring that the web address is included prominently on traditional print media (i.e., direct mail, notices on statements, etc.). Include your web address in all your traditional employment advertisements. It's really a matter of being consistent about your marketing and using a number of different vehicles to market.

Most important, make sure that your listings are up to date, and that you're responsive to the inquiries that you do receive.

2. Other Sources of Applicants

New media aren't the only source of job applicants when searching for telecommuters. The traditional media may work well, depending on your specific needs. Placing classified ads in local newspapers or running ads in related trade journals can be effective ways of reaching potential telecommuting candidates. In fact, Tom Joseph, president and CEO of Bookminders — a company that provides bookkeeping services with a staff made up exclusively of home-based workers — uses classified ads in the local paper to attract candidates. He has been so successful using this traditional recruiting source that, even during times when the economy is soaring, he has been able to reach the point where he has had an overabundance of applicants. His success in attracting candidates speaks well to the growing interest in flexible work options. "We're attracting people who want to work out of their homes, which includes a lot of people," Joseph says. "We've come to see our recruiting as a sort of filtering process."

Other sources of applicants include:

- *Job fairs.* Job fairs are becoming an increasingly popular source of job candidates. Generally organized by industry, job fairs are like trade shows that provide employers with the opportunity to meet interested job seekers in a particular field. For instance, a community might sponsor a small-manufacturing job fair at which area manufacturers would be present to provide information on their companies and their personnel needs.

Although using the Internet can certainly help you to reach a broad pool of talent, don't abandon traditional methods such as newspaper classified ads, job fairs, and employee referrals.

- *Recruitment open houses.* Holding an open house for your own company provides you with the opportunity to present your job openings exclusively to a group of interested job candidates.

- *Recommendations and referrals.* Referrals from your existing employees can be a great source of potential telecommuting candidates. These referrals can generally be trusted — after all, the employee has a vested interest in seeing the referral work out.

Rather than relying on any one source for applicants, use a combination of means to generate interest. Whatever means you use, be sure to clearly outline your needs and expectations. The recruitment stage is the critical first step toward ensuring that your telecommuters will be capable and productive.

3. Steps in the Hiring Process

Whether advertising in the local paper, running an ad on Monster.com, or "trolling" for employees on a social media site, the hiring process you use for telecommuters will be much the same as for any employee.

3.1 Position requirements

As with any position, your first step in hiring a telecommuter will be determining the requirements of the position. This will not only help you make an informed decision, but will also help narrow your choices in terms of recruitment vehicles. Before you begin your search, you should consider the following:

- *Education.* What level of education is necessary to perform effectively in the position? High school? College? Special training? Will job performance require any type of special certificate or license?

- *Experience.* How much previous, related experience should a new employee have? Will training be offered on the job? Experience and education requirements are often tied together; for example, "Bachelor's degree plus a minimum of three years' experience in the field."

- *Personality requirements.* As discussed in Chapter 4, there are specific personality traits that differentiate those who will perform effectively as telecommuters from those who will not be successful in this role.

As you put together your list of requirements, make sure that each is specifically job related to avoid claims or charges of discrimination. Don't make these job determinations in a vacuum. Ask other members of the organization for their perspectives.

Be specific. Communication is a critical element in any telecommuting relationship, and it starts during recruitment. You should have a very clear understanding of what the job will entail and the specific requirements of the position. Job descriptions and job specifications are two tools that can greatly help you in this process.

Outlining your expectations before hiring an individual will allow you to evaluate his or her performance fairly.

The job description provides a written record of the qualifications required for the position and outlines how the job relates to others in the company. It should include —

- position title,
- salary or pay grade,
- department,
- to whom the position is accountable,
- hours required,
- job summary,
- major responsibilities or tasks,
- qualifications, and
- relation of the position to others in the company.

The job description should be organized in such a way that it indicates not only the responsibilities involved, but also the relative importance of these responsibilities. The telecommuting job description should also indicate how the telecommuter will interact with colleagues, and should discuss other issues related to the telecommuting relationship. Within the broad categories mentioned above, you will want to include such information as —

- extent of authority exercised over the position,
- level of complexity of the duties performed,
- amount of internal and external contact (including any requirements for on-site meetings),
- amount of access to confidential information,
- amount of independent judgment required,
- amount of pressure involved in the job,

- type of equipment used (and how that equipment will be purchased and maintained),
- working conditions (including expectations for the home office environment), and
- terms of employment.

Job specifications are another useful tool in the recruitment process. Job specifications describe the personal qualifications that are required for a job and include any special conditions of employment. In the case of telecommuting, this may include such things as required hours of availability and responsibility for maintaining equipment.

Some key questions to ask yourself as you are preparing a position description are the following:

- What is the purpose of the job?
- What day-to-day duties are performed?
- How is the position supervised?
- What other positions receive supervision from this position?
- How much, or how little, control is exercised over this position?
- What machines or equipment must be operated?
- What types of records need to be kept by this position?
- To what extent is this position involved in analysis and planning?
- What internal and external contacts are required of this position?
- What verbal, numerical, or mechanical aptitudes are required?

3.2 Selection criteria

On what evidence will you base your hiring decision? There are three commonly used selection measures for evaluating job applicants, including self-report, direct observation, and work samples. You may decide to use one or a combination of all three.

Self-report is the most commonly used measure. You ask the applicant about their accomplishments and experience, and they provide you with information — information that is, by its very nature, subject to bias. Direct observation, although often not possible, allows you to actually observe the candidate doing the work you will require. To approximate this measure, you might —

- use one of many tests that have been developed to measure various skills and abilities,

- role-play certain tasks (i.e., sales calls, telemarketing scripts, etc.), or

- use hypothetical questions or situations to approximate real-life situations.

Work samples are appropriate for a number of positions that might lend themselves to telecommuting (i.e., computer programmers, website developers, writers, graphic designers).

The job specifications that you used to begin your job search will play a major role in helping you make a final decision. Applicants should be evaluated both in terms of how well they meet the job specifications and how they compare to other applicants. For this reason, it is important to reserve a final decision until all interviews have been completed. Don't make a decision after each interview. It is best to wait until all interviews are completed and then rate interviewees on the basis of the criteria you have determined are the best predictors of job performance.

The selection process is subjective, leaving many areas open to bias and error. If you are aware of the possibility for error, you have taken one of the first steps to becoming a fair evaluator of job applicants. The following points can help make this demanding task a little less intimidating:

- Be prepared

- Identify desired behaviors in observable rather than subjective terms

- Be aware of your own personal biases and work to overcome them

- Try using more than one interviewer and comparing results to determine possible bias

- Don't assume that excellence in one area implies excellence in all areas

- Base judgments on demonstrated performance, not anticipated performance

3.3 Interviewing candidates for off-site jobs

Interviewing candidates for remote work can be done far more conveniently and creatively than one might imagine. For example, your first interview might actually take place online, via email. After all, if this is

Since about one-third of all job applicants alter their résumés or misrepresent their qualifications, it is vital that you take the time to check references.

the means by which you will most frequently communicate with your telecommuting employee, doesn't it make sense to get a good idea of their skills in this medium up front? From there, you may want to go on to a telephone interview. Eventually, but not always, you may want to bring the candidate into your office.

The interview process will be much the same as the process for hiring any employee. Focus on the criteria you've established for the position and develop questions designed to determine if the candidates have the experience, background, and personal traits and characteristics that will enable them to be successful telecommuters.

Your goal is to identify behaviors that will lead to successful job performance and to devise questions that let you determine if applicants will be a good fit. Project yourself into the future. Look back and describe the ideal outcome. This gives you a sense of what a good person to hire "looks like."

When you ask questions of your telecommuting candidates, you want to gather as much information as possible and probe for meaningful responses. Your interviewing skills will determine whether or not you gather all the pertinent information.

While there are never any guarantees that the person you hire will work out, a well-conducted interview will improve your chances of making an informed decision.

3.4 References

About a third of all job candidates alter their résumés or misrepresent their qualifications when applying for a job.

Ninety percent of all hiring mistakes can be prevented through proper reference-checking procedures. Unfortunately, countless employers neglect this important step in the hiring process. They rely instead on their own impressions of the candidate based on the résumé, application, and interview. This is a major mistake and it can be a costly one. Checking the references of your telecommuting applicants is absolutely essential to obtain accurate information about their qualifications and experience.

Many employers call references after interviews have been conducted. Making these calls beforehand can help you filter out undesirable candidates earlier, saving time that you would have spent in an interview. Checking references before the interview can also provide you with additional areas to explore during the interview, and can help you formulate pertinent questions in advance.

Before checking references, prepare questions and have a clear idea of the information you hope to obtain. You will want to ask questions related to the applicant's ability to work independently, to be productive, and to achieve results. Keep in mind that some organizations have policies against giving a great deal of information about former or current employees and will provide little detail beyond length of service and rate of pay. Still, it pays to be persistent and to ask for additional sources of information along the way. Try asking, "Is there anyone else I should speak with?"

Try these questions when checking references:

- What was the quality of the applicant's work?

- How much direction did the applicant need?

- Did the applicant consistently meet deadlines?

- How were the applicant's problem-solving skills?

- Tell me about the applicant's communication skills.

- In your opinion, is this a person who can work well in a telecommuting position with minimal supervision?

4. Perils and Pitfalls

Any hiring decision is important, but when hiring telecommuters, you must be particularly vigilant. Because you will be relying upon them to be self-sufficient and reliable, you need to make sure that you take the time to clearly identify the type of candidate you need, to interview carefully, to check references, and to make hiring decisions based on objective criteria. There are a number of potential perils and pitfalls that you should be aware of as you go through this process:

- *Not adapting your processes and procedures to the online environment.* The world is changing, technology is changing, and your hiring practices need to change too. Many of the steps you have taken in the past will not convert readily — or efficiently — to online venues. Be flexible and willing to adapt whenever necessary.

- *Limiting yourself to one or two sources of applicants.* Don't give up on traditional sources of recruiting, such as newspapers or trade journals. Take advantage of the plethora of recruitment sites, and keep up with the new additions. Be adventurous and be constantly alert to new online opportunities.

- *Overlooking local or regional sites.* Local communities frequently have job-site listings at chamber of commerce or local newspaper sites. If you're located in Minnesota, but want to tap into the technological expertise you believe exists in San Francisco, check out some of the local San Francisco sites in addition to the major national sites.

- *Not using the sites yourself.* The best way to learn about recruitment over the Internet is to actively visit and use the various sites. As a user you can test the search capabilities, posting opportunities, content, and general usability of these sites.

- *Comparing apples to oranges.* One of the benefits — and downfalls — of the Internet is that even the least experienced and least reputable organizations can develop sites that present a "Wow!" image. Don't be too easily taken in by the glamorous front. Carefully consider the types of postings the site offers, the number of postings, and the charges (direct and hidden) before making any decision to pay for services.

5. Case Study

Bookminders, Inc. was founded in 1991 to provide outsourced bookkeeping services to 150 companies and nonprofit groups, and has drawn much attention as a model for off-site success. Bookminders is unique, in a sense, because it was conceived with the intention that "home-based workers would drive" the business. Bookminders targets small- to medium-sized businesses that require at least part-time bookkeeping support. The company offers all the benefits of an in-house computer bookkeeping department without the support burden or cost overhead, and serves more than 150 different businesses, including contractors, consultants, restaurants, retailers, manufacturers, medical professionals, lawyers, nonprofits, and property managers. "We've grown and now have offices in two cities and are on the cusp of licensing our model to firms in other markets," says Tom Joseph, founder and CEO of Bookminders.

All of Bookminders' employees work from home and communicate with the office via fax and email. Most workers are women with young children and work between 20 and 40 hours a week. The home of each employee is equipped with hardware, software, and communication equipment that links the workforce with the corporate office.

Joseph says that through trial and error, he believes he has found a process that works for finding employees. The extensive amount of training and orientation involved for Bookminders staff means that the investment of time in any one employee can be substantial. Joseph can't afford to have high turnover. Consequently, he must make sure that his hiring practices are sound.

It all starts with an ad in the local newspaper. Ads are run each month and generally elicit 20 to 30 applicants. Applicants are invited to an open house — a structured event — where, Joseph says, "we basically try to talk them out of working for us." The reasons are simple. According to Joseph, he does not suffer from a lack of job applicants. On the contrary, he receives an overabundance of résumés. He has found that to reduce the applicants to a chosen few, it is important to first of all be very specific in the recruitment ads; second, to clearly outline to prospective employees what the requirements of the job will be; and third, to implement a process of testing designed to weed through the remaining applicants. In fact, Joseph says, anywhere from one-third to one-half of his applicants are not able to pass the tests he gives — and those applicants are accounting professionals with college degrees and three to five years of experience.

Joseph wants only the best candidates, so the application process must be rigorous. "If our recruiting process isn't working, it's expensive," he says. "That's why we put a ton of time into this process."

Because Tom Joseph, CEO of Bookminders, receives an overabundance of résumés, he has developed an extensive recruitment process designed to ensure that only the best-suited applicants are hired.

Chapter 6
TRAINING OFF-SITE WORKERS AND THEIR MANAGERS

"[Training] improve[s] the quality of the telecommuting program by taking the guesswork out of remote work."

— Gil Gordon, founder of consulting firm Gil Gordon Associates

Executive Summary

Is training really necessary?

Training is critical! But don't stop with just training your remote workers. Training should also be offered for managers — and even for traditional, on-site employees who will be required to interact with their off-site colleagues.

How much training should I offer?

Enough to cover the key points — to provide employees and managers with the information they need to make this relationship a success. Training times vary from one- to two-hour sessions to one- to three-day sessions. It all depends on your particular situation. The key is not to skimp on training.

Do managers need training?

Yes. In fact, in addition to individual sessions, it's a good idea to offer an opportunity for managers and employees to have the opportunity to spend time with each other to discuss the details of the arrangement.

Can managers really be trained to supervise off-site staff and telecommuters?

Yes. While the skills required to effectively manage off-site staff and telecommuters are very similar to those required to manage any employee, there are specific techniques and interactions that are unique to these relationships. Chief among these is the ability to manage based on outcomes rather than on process. Managers need to become comfortable with the concept of managing employees who are not physically present. The establishment of clear expectations and frequent communication become a critical part of this relationship. These are issues that can be successfully dealt with through training and education.

Is an initial training session sufficient?

It's a good start. But, refresher sessions can be helpful, particularly as technology changes. Other issues (work schedules, goals, etc.) should be covered regularly as part of your normal evaluation and review process.

Can training be done online?

Yes. Today's technology make it both economical and efficient to offer training online through a variety of means including webinars, video, interactive forums, etc. Reference materials can readily be placed online for quick and easy access by remote workers.

TRAINING OFF-SITE WORKERS AND THEIR MANAGERS

"While companies and workers are readily embracing telecommuting, many employers are not taking on the responsibility of properly equipping, training, or providing protections for their telecommuters," says Dr. Charlie Grantham of the Institute for the Study of Distributed Work, which offers consulting services for Fortune 500 companies entering the alternative work world.

"This is really a leadership opportunity for employers," Grantham says. "As the workplace becomes more mobile, employers need to think about extending support to telecommuters — not just from a productivity standpoint, but also to address liability questions and to stay ahead of guidelines that may be otherwise legislated."

As we've already discussed, teleworkers are not the only off-site staff that could benefit from training related to how they can be most effective and productive in remote locations. Whether working from a home office, a branch office, or on an international assignment, the ability to communicate effectively, and use the tools that the organization has available to expedite work processes, is critical.

To be most effective, training should be considered, from the very beginning, as a program or process that allows workers to work from locations other than the main office. The policies and procedures related

To make a telecommuting program successful, a training program should be developed as soon as possible.

to these work relationships can form the basis of much of the training, says George Piskurich, author of *An Organizational Guide to Telecommuting* (ASTD, 1998). "In the act of conceptualizing a telecommuting program and defining policies and procedures to institute in your company, you have already taken a major step in creating a solid training program," he says. He maintains that "those policies and procedures — what they are, what they mean, and how to work within them — are 50 percent to 60 percent of the training."

Companies that have been working with off-site employees for some time have incorporated training into the process, recognizing its importance. In many of these companies, training is broken down into three parts: training for employees; training for supervisors/managers; and "team training" — that is, outlining opportunities for the employee and his or her manager to come together and discuss the issues that impact the relationship. This three-tiered training structure is an essential tool for implementing and maintaining relationships that work. Let's have a closer look at how these three facets of training operate.

1. Employee Training

Successful off-site work relationships don't just happen because an employee who used to work in the office now works from home. It's not quite that simple. There are certain differences between working at the head office and working at home. Those differences need to be covered through training and orientation to ensure that the employee knows what to expect and is capable of making the transition.

1.1 Characteristics of employee training programs

Employee training programs generally have the following characteristics:

- Individual sessions are conducted for employees and their managers; both groups are brought together at some point to participate in planning and general discussion.

- Technology is an element of training, but it takes a back seat to more critical issues such as a heavy emphasis on communication skills, establishment of measurable goals, and discussion of how to measure progress.

- A focus on some of the "softer" issues such as how to deal with interruptions at home and how to handle isolation, and a sharing of experiences are important parts of the training process.

Dr. Richard A. Skinner, president of Clayton College & State University and the Metropolitan Atlanta Telecommuting Advisory Council, says, "We've found that the training begins with the workers and managers together initially so they all hear the same thing. We've found that small groups work best — about 20 people. And we've found that what we call the sharing opportunity — people talking through their experiences — is important. I call this testimonial time. You can have all of the slick films and presentation you want, but what people want to hear are authentic voices."

Steve Schilling of TeleCommute Solutions says that a mistake that many companies make when it comes to telecommuting training is that they "train on technology, but they don't get into the basic experience-type things or the coordination-type things. When you're implementing a telecommuting program, step one is to understand that there are a lot of issues at play beyond technology and that the cultural, managerial, and interpersonal implications of telecommuting are really much bigger than technology."

By separating technology from the core training, organizations are able to focus on more critical issues, such as communication. "Communication skills are the core," Grantham says. "When you start to substitute email and voicemail for face-to-face conversations, communication gets a little bit muddier, a little bit messier."

Steve Schilling emphasizes that training needs to go beyond technology training to address the human issues of telecommuting.

1.2 A structure for training

Gil Gordon has developed some training programs that are structured on some very basic principles, and have proven to be highly effective.

The training, he says, should become "institutionalized" — "as routine as any other training that you'd expect to happen normally in an organization. That means that it's offered not once, but on some regular interval." As do others, he views the role of HR as critical. "If I had my wish, the ideal training faculty would be a team: a line manager who could speak from experience, a real telecommuter, and an HR or training person. That provides the combination of real-life experience and peers talking to peers against the backdrop of a training professional."

Sample 3 is a summary of Gordon's program for telecommuters.

SAMPLE 3
SAMPLE OUTLINE FOR A TELECOMMUTING TRAINING PROGRAM

BRIEFING SESSION FOR PROSPECTIVE TELECOMMUTERS

PURPOSE: To help prospective telecommuters make an informed decision about whether or not they want to apply for consideration to be selected into a telecommuting pilot program. Also useful for people considering working at home in a more informal program. The objective is to make sure the people look beyond some of the obvious advantages (e.g., more flexible schedule, less formal environment, better family interaction, less commuting) and consider some of the special demands and requirements of working at home.

FORMAT: A 90-minute session that begins with a short overview about telecommuting (unless this has been provided already). Next, a short self-scoring survey to help employees identify how well they are likely to succeed as telecommuters, based on issues of suitability of the home setting, support from family members, relationship with the supervisor, and other factors.

This is followed by an interactive discussion of "Ten Key Questions" that prospective telecommuters should ask themselves about working at home, and then a candid discussion of the real and perceived career effects of working as a telecommuter. Also reviewed are the role of and content of the "telecommuter's agreement," and a series of "Next Steps" to be taken before deciding whether or not to request participation as a telecommuter.

BENEFITS TO PARTICIPANTS: This session improves the quality of the telecommuting program by:

- Helping employees who are not suited for telecommuting screen themselves out of consideration

- Helping employers keep the cost of training and equipping telecommuters down by eliminating employees who are less likely to succeed as telecommuters

- Creating enthusiasm for the telecommuting concept, while adding some much-needed reality to the myths that often exist

- The session can be run with groups of 10–30 participants; larger groups are possible but this limits the valuable discussion and interaction.

(Copyright© 1998, Gil Gordon Associates.)

1.3 Making it real

All of the training in the world and all possible interaction with experienced off-site workers can't substitute for personal experience. The transition from office to an alternative location is a trying one for many, and companies struggle with ways to make the move less stressful and more productive.

The more closely a training program can approximate an off-site experience, the better.

Bernadette Fusaro is a work/life manager for Merrill Lynch, where she is responsible for the organization's alternative work programs, including telecommuting. Fusaro points to their simulation lab as a unique aspect of training that really makes a difference for employees making the transition to telecommuting. The lab is a large room that contains work stations where telecommuters work for two weeks, using the equipment that they will bring home with them. At the end of the two-week period, they're taught how to put their computers together and take them apart, then they're given the computers to take home to work. "We've found that that's been an excellent way to prepare telecommuters," Fusaro says.

Technology can definitely assist in the training process, George Piskurich says. He tells of a training program his company did with a client that involved a computer-mediated instruction process. Instead of having participants come to the classroom, they were hooked up through their company's intranet. "Trainees and instructors did the whole thing as if they were telecommuters," Piskurich says. "We put together files they had to share and things they had to do. It all revolved around the processes of telecommuting — sharing what your ten greatest fears are, a file on how to overcome problems of workaholism. We gave them a taste of what it's like to be a telecommuter. They never saw anybody else." Grantham offers a caveat to this approach, though. "I don't think people can be trained to be teleworkers on the Internet," he says. "It needs to be a face-to-face, interactive environment."

Your approach must be tailored to the specific needs of your business. You may find that some combination of face-to-face instruction with the opportunity to work alone in an environment that simulates what the telecommuter will face in his or her home is optimum.

2. Supervisor/Manager Training

Your efforts to allow for alternative work arrangements will fall apart very quickly if you train only the employees and not their managers. You will not only have to be concerned with implementing a revised management structure and approach for people who manage remote staff. Your first challenge will be to overcome the prevailing attitudes

Dr. Grantham points out that managers may have concerns about being undervalued if they were to manage teleworkers.

and fears that your managers may have toward employees who are "out of sight."

2.1 An unnerving transition for managers

The resistance of supervisors and managers is a common barrier to implementing alternative work arrangements, and one that must be tackled head-on at an early stage in the process.

"Very often, supervisors are afraid," says George Piskurich. "They think it's going to put them out of business." But in reality, Piskurich points out, "if you have a lot of off-site staff, you need even better supervisory skills."

In an employment environment marked by downsizing and a continuing emphasis on cost-cutting, this fear is understandable. It is this fear, Dr. Grantham believes, that is at the basis of most managers' hesitance to embrace the concept of remote workers. "The typical 'If I can't see them, how do I know they're working?' attitude really is a red herring, I believe. What I've found at the core of the concern for managers really turns out to be their uncertainty, or concern that they won't be valued by the company if they're managing people who aren't physically on site." Grantham tells of a manager who once told him that the boss came out of his office, looked at all of the empty cubicles and said, "What do I need you for?" This, Grantham believes, really gets at the heart of the hesitation that many managers feel.

A certain anxiety regarding management technique can crop up as well. This is where a solid training program is most vital for managers. Learning to make the transition from managing time to managing projects is a critical shift for most managers. "One of the key challenges for managers," says Roger Herman, strategic business futurist, CEO of the Herman Group in Greensboro and author of *Keeping Good People*, "is the shift from activity-based management to results-based management. You're not going to know if that person's sitting at their desk at 8:00 a.m., or how many breaks they're taking." In a telecommuting relationship, time is not the most important factor.

These are major shifts in the traditional approach to managing. How do you manage people you can't see? How do you measure performance if not by hours worked?

2.2 A structure for supervisory training

"I think managers often believe that they know more about managing and are more competent at it than they really are," says Gil Gordon.

"This has been the curse of every training person to walk the face of the earth. How do you stimulate some interest without wanting to intimidate or browbeat them?" Gordon approaches this issue by —

- Teaching managers that "everything they have been doing so far is not wrong and that there is not some brand new theory of management that must be adopted where they have to learn all new jargon and so on."

- Focusing on the basics. "The essence of training for the manager is to stay focused on those good, old-fashioned Management 101 topics that managers have always been talked to about, but that most managers get away from doing because they have the luxury of frequent close contact in the office."

"My approach for the training," says Gordon, "is mostly a matter of fine-tuning what we hope they're already doing and maybe introducing some new concepts, as opposed to starting from scratch, which is not necessary and which will not gain many fans."

The message is: Keep it simple. You don't need to create chaos among your managers. You simply need to look at the employee-manager relationship and address the basic issues. As Roger Herman points out, even training on such simple skills as how to communicate effectively over the phone or by email can have a positive impact on the relationship. "One of the things the supervisor has to be sensitive to, of course, is maintaining that high level of communication, keeping them involved and realizing that managing someone you can't see is considerably different than walking around the cubicle wall to see that they're there at 8:00 in the morning."

An important part of this process, then, is recognizing exactly what about the employee-manager relationship will need to be addressed. Many of these details will inevitably arise as you are working toward implementing your program, but it is a good idea to have a planned period of observation and assessment before you begin.

Bernadette Fusaro provides a service to managers called process consultation. "We will go into an area and identify for the manager ahead of time what the barriers will be to implementing flexibility," she says. "We look at the way employees communicate. We look at areas that will potentially be problems before we even introduce it to employees." This groundwork helps to alleviate concerns that managers may have and also identifies specific areas that need to be addressed as the work arrangement is formalized.

Telecommuters and their managers need to attend a joint training meeting in which they develop objectives and work out all the minor details in advance.

Gil Gordon's manager training program for managers of telecommuters is a two-hour session designed to "improve the quality of the telecommuting program by taking the guesswork out of remote work, and making sure that everyone has thought through the critical issues." The following topics are covered:

- Managing by results instead of by observation
- Fine-tuning skills for setting performance standards and giving ongoing performance feedback
- Keeping telecommuters linked to the office
- Career management issues for telecommuters
- Spotting problems early and dealing with them effectively

The techniques of remote management are discussed in detail in Chapter 7.

CHECKLIST 2
SUPERVISOR'S CHECKLIST FOR TELECOMMUTERS
(CALIFORNIA DEPARTMENT OF PERSONNEL ADMINISTRATION)

Name of telecommuter _____

Name of supervisor _____

Date completed _____

☐ Employee has read the orientation documents and the telecommuting policy.

☐ Employee has been provided with a schedule of core hours or guidelines for flexing work hours.

☐ Equipment issued is documented.

☐ Performance expectations have been discussed and are clearly understood. Assignments and due dates are documented.

☐ Requirements for adequate and safe office space at home have been reviewed with the employee and the employee certifies that those requirements have been met.

☐ Requirements for care of equipment assigned to the employee have been discussed and are clearly understood.

☐ The employee is familiar with the requirements and techniques for computer information security and has received a copy and read the Information Security Guidelines.

☐ Phone contact procedures have been clearly defined and unit secretaries and receptionists have received training.

☐ The employee has read and signed the Telecommuter's Agreement prior to actual participation in the program.

2.3 Supervisor's checklist

As part of the training and orientation process for managers, it can be helpful to offer some specific information on expectations for the management process, or helpful tips that can aid managers in effectively overseeing their telecommuters.

The California Department of Personnel Administration's "Supervisor's Checklist for Telecommuters" (reproduced here as Checklist 2) was designed to start the relationship on a basis of mutual understanding and ensure that all the details of the arrangement have been covered.

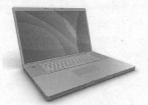

Training for a telecommuting program should include the entire organization, not just off-site staff. All staff should be aware of how telecommuting will affect them.

3. Team Training

It's not enough to hold training sessions for telecommuters and then hold training sessions for their managers. At some point along the way, these two groups need to be brought together. "The employee has to understand what the supervisor's problems are going to be, and vice versa," Piskurich points out.

At Merrill Lynch, joint sessions are used as a forum for discussion as well as an opportunity to develop objectives. "The employees bring their work objectives, and the manager and employee sit down and discuss the expectations of the arrangement," Fusaro says. "The manager will talk about when he or she expects the employee to be available and what kind of communication they will use. They iron out ahead of time how this arrangement is going to work. That's a big step because things are not left to chance."

"The joint sessions, I find the most interesting," says Gordon, "and attendees do too. It's really a negotiating and planning session." At these sessions Gordon asks employees and managers to discuss such basic issues as "How many days a week are you going to work off-site?", "Which days will they be?", and "How often will you check email?".

"As mundane as these questions may seem," he says, "I have seen over and over again that if they are not discussed in advance, you wind up with two very different sets of expectations that are really pretty dangerous when they come up against each other."

Gordon's telecommuter training programs schedule the joint session as the final session, after the telecommuters and their managers have undergone training separately. The topics covered in this joint discussion session include the following:

- Detailing the schedule, availability, phone coverage, and office days

- Planning the first few weeks of telecommuting
- Minimizing effects on department workflow
- Providing technical (equipment) support as needed
- Dealing with system shutdowns and other problems

4. Training the Rest of the Staff

The workforce at large also needs to have some training and education to familiarize them with the alternative work arrangements that are part of the company's operations. "If the entire organization isn't trained and educated about alternative work options — how it's being implemented, who is being selected and why — then folks that aren't even involved in it can be impacted in negative ways in terms of losing touch with people in the program," says Steve Schilling.

But the training challenge doesn't stop here. There's yet another important group that must be considered. Grantham stresses that executive education is another element of preparedness. Too often, he says, "the vice presidents and other administrators will say the company supports it, and then disappear. They're not really as sensitive, I think, as they need to be to what's going on. They need some education, too."

In addition to up-front education, Grantham typically brings the executive staff back into the process about six months into the program, using productivity measurements as the basis for business case analysis. "We bring it back to the executives in terms of what impact it's having on productivity, cost, and customer satisfaction. That usually makes believers out of them."

5. After Training

It's important, Gordon says, to plan training sessions as close as possible to the actual time when off-site work assignments will begin. "I think training creates some momentum, some excitement, and it's a shame to waste that. It's like teaching somebody how to play golf and then they don't get to go out on the golf course for six months. No matter how good the training is, people either just forget it or they tend to lose that edge."

Are potential off-site employees ever discouraged from telecommuting after they go through the training process? It happens. "We had some people who, after the training, said, 'This is not for me,'" Fusaro recalls. "But it's been minimal. We've had a few people who have been home for a while and said, 'I miss the interaction.'" But, she says, for the most part, "the ones that go through the training like it, and we've had very little fallout."

6. Tips for Starting Telecommuters

Steve Schilling and Telecommute Solutions offer the following tips for telecommuters. These are concerns that should be addressed in your telecommuting training program and should become fundamental to the way in which your program operates:

- *Face time is very important.* If you are a regular telecommuter, use your day at the office for face-to-face meetings and plain old human connections. Don't be afraid to ask for meeting agendas and starting and ending times. You can nicely let people know that your time in the office is limited so you need to manage it carefully. After just a few meetings, they will realize that your time is important and will not waste it. We have found that meetings that involve telecommuters are more effective and more productive than those made up of office staffers only.

- *The biggest mistake is to hide behind email or voice mail.* Staying in touch with your manager or coworkers is one of the most important things that you can do for yourself. Don't rely on days in the office to provide the human touch. By cultivating and nourishing your relationships with your coworkers, you can stay informed of important developments within the company and have friends you can call on if you need support. The fear of invisibility will not be an issue if you continue to communicate; and the responsibility to do so is yours!

- *Share knowledge and expertise.* As a telecommuter, you should add as much to the equation from a home office as from the enterprise office. The second biggest mistake you can make is to let non-telecommuting colleagues believe that you are a casual worker. By your words and deeds, let everyone know that they should expect the same standard of work from you as from office workers.

- *Be aware of jealousy and misconceptions.* Don't brag about your lack of commuting or any other of the benefits you have discovered about telecommuting. While you don't have to lie about the benefits and rewards of telecommuting, we suggest that you tell the truth when asked but don't keep telling everyone at the office how lucky you are.

7. Case Study

Sun Microsystems, Inc., with corporate headquarters in Santa Clara, California, provides a diverse array of software, systems, services, and microelectronics that power everything — from consumer electronics to developer tools and the world's most powerful datacenters. A technology company, Sun long ago learned to use its own technology to allow employees to work from virtually any place they choose. It has been offering flexible work options since 1995.

In fact, when its "open work" program was established, new hires were allowed to decide where they preferred to work when they negotiated their offer letter.

Sun employees can work how, when and where they personally will feel most productive, creative, innovative and inspired. As Sun says, "the whole world is their office." At the end of 2008, 20,000 employees representing more than 56 percent of the workforce were working away from the office at least one or two days a week. But at Sun, everyone is considered an "open worker," living the philosophy that "it's what you do, not where you do it, that counts." The program is not about working from home or working from the office. It's about having the tools to work wherever skills and knowledge can be most effectively employed, Sun says.

This flexibility, according to Sun, enables:

- Better work/life balance

- More efficient and effective use of time

- Greater flexibility in planning work and meetings

- Reduced stress from commutes

- Saved commuting time — an average of 104 hours per year, the equivalent of two-and-a-half weeks of vacation

- Employee gasoline expense savings of $870/year

Sun has achieved measurable savings through its open work practices:

- A reduction in real estate holdings of more than 15 percent (2.6 million square feet) in 2007 and lowered real estate operating costs.

- Flexible employees' initial and annual workspace expenses are about 30 percent lower than those of employees assigned to a fixed office.

- Home assigned employees' initial and annual workplace expenses are about 70 percent less than fixed-office employees.

Sun has also achieved real-world sustainability benefits from its open work practices. It was able to quickly respond to both the 2003 SARS outbreak and 2007 California fires.

Employees benefit in a real way as well. In addition to time and money saved on commuting, Sun's 2008 Annual All Employee Survey results indicated that two of the top reasons 82 percent of employees said they would recommend Sun were its work environment and ability to attract and retain top talent.

Sun's efforts also benefit the environment and it has been recognized for these efforts. Sun is among the top ten Fortune 500 companies that lead the country by providing outstanding commuter benefits to a significant portion of its US workforce, to help decrease air pollution, traffic congestion, and dependence on fossil fuels.

Of course, technology helps companies make telecommuting possible. Sun asks remote employees to report to work through a virtual private network and a virtual desktop using a secure Java-enabled card ID. Files are stored on a central server rather than individual PCs. Sun has established a consulting practice to help other businesses set up similar virtual workspace programs.

The top ten myths about flexible work options that Sun works to overcome include:

- If employees sign up for mobile work, on-site staff will never see them again.

- Managers and team members will lose direct contact with remote employees.

- Productivity will suffer if employees work remotely from home.

- Teams can't be productive if they don't sit together.

- Employees prefer traditional work arrangements.

- Implementing a mobile work program will cost too much.

- Only technically savvy employees can work remotely.

- Working remotely adversely affects career advancement. If employees aren't physically present, their job security and opportunities for career advancement will suffer.

- Remote work won't work for a certain business.

- If managers allow mobile work, they will lose control.

- Mobile work won't have any measurable impact on employee attraction and retention.

Chapter 7
MANAGING
OFF-SITE STAFF

"Developing a results-oriented system for managing performance is fundamental to successful supervision of a home worker."

— Tom Joseph, Bookminders, Inc.

Executive Summary

What if one of my employees wants to work from home and I don't think that employee would be a good candidate for off-site work?

Your decision of whether or not to allow an employee to work in a non-traditional or off-site work arrangement should be based on objective criteria that are widely communicated to employees. Not every employee will be a good candidate for off-site work with limited supervision, and you should not feel obligated to allow any employee to do so.

How can I keep track of what my off-site employees are doing?

The same way you should be keeping track of what any of your employees are doing. Your staff should be judged on the outcomes of their work, not on the processes used to obtain results. Work with each employee to identify specific job-related expectations and objectives. Criteria might include the quantity of work output, quality of work output, and adherence to deadlines.

What will the impact on employees and customers be when I have off-site employees on my staff?

The needs of customers — both external and internal — are extremely important and should be foremost in your mind when allowing flexible work arrangements or establishing a formal telecommuting program. There should be either no impact, or a positive impact. If there is the potential for a negative impact, these arrangements should not be an option.

How can I deal with the social-interaction needs of off-site staff?

Isolation can be a very real issue for off-site staff, but there are a number of ways to help these employees maintain their positions as part of the work team.

Regularly scheduled days in the office, frequent communication, and scheduled events and meetings are all methods that managers and companies have used to maintain interaction and to ensure that off-site employees do not become invisible or forgotten.

What if some supervisors allow employees to work off-site and others don't?

For these flexible work arrangements to be effective, managers must be behind the effort. While some companies implement formal telecommuting programs across the organization, many leave the decision up to individual managers. Hesitant managers should be encouraged to make their decisions based on the unique requirements of the positions in their departments and the skills and capabilities of employees.

What if the arrangement just doesn't work?

There is always the chance that the arrangement will not work out — for you or for the employee. This is an issue that should be addressed in the initial agreement. As with any other employee-performance situation, you should be prepared to address this issue quickly and directly if it comes up.

MANAGING OFF-SITE STAFF

Even when managers have direct line-of-sight contact with members of their staff, managing employees can be a challenge. Many managers become managers because of their expertise in their field, without having any formal management training. Frequently, they learn through trial and error. It's not surprising, then, that managers often balk at nontraditional work arrangements. Managing is hard enough without the added stress and uncertainty of trying to keep track of people who aren't even in the building! As discussed in Chapter 6, managers are often reluctant or wary when it comes to the consideration of work arrangements in which employees are "out of sight." Misconceptions abound, and these misconceptions can prevent alternative work arrangements from developing, or sabotage them once they're in place. But what managers sometimes don't realize is that allowing employees flexibility in their schedules and work locations can easily become a win-win situation, improving manager-employee relations, management techniques and effectiveness, and productivity.

1. The Truth about Managing Off-site Staff

Good managers are good managers — whether supervising employees who work in the same physical location they do, or supervising employees in remote locations. Basic management tools are just as important

Since telecommuters cannot be visually supervised, they must be evaluated on the attainment of goals.

for remote staff as they are for people in the office, but you may need to tailor your supervision for those working at home. "Management by Walking Around" won't work. You'll probably find that you need to focus more on results than appearance. Scheduling might get tricky. And you'll be called upon to show trust and support to employees who are working remotely — and to those who are not.

Results are what count — not face time, putting in long hours, working "overtime," or any of the other "traditional" ways of measuring performance. This is much the same as any other type of management except it truly tests your skills. It requires an added level of communication, more carefully crafted and measurable objectives, and clear and direct feedback.

One of the questions posed by interviewers who prepared the report "Moving Telecommuting Forward: An Examination of Organizational Variables" (July 1999), the result of an extensive study of twelve managers of telecommuters conducted at the National Center for Transportation and Industrial Productivity at the New Jersey Institute of Technology (NJIT), was: "How is productivity measured for telecommuters?"

According to the report, the managers of telecommuters, who also managed non-telecommuters, reported in all instances that productivity measurement was similar for both. Goal achievement was mentioned most frequently, followed by work timeliness, contract and sales, work accuracy, cost efficiency, and, in one instance, publications. What is notable about all of these measures, according to the report, is that they focus on work outcomes and not on work process. It's not how the work gets done that matters, it's what gets done that counts.

2. Traits of Successful Remote Managers

The traits of successful managers of off-site workers are actually no different from the traits of any successful managers — with the exception, perhaps, of a heightened need for excellence in communication, goal setting, and providing feedback.

TeleCommute Solutions, Inc. asked current managers of telecommuters to identify which attributes of management they considered most important. More than 50 percent of these managers identified adequate planning skills as a critical requirement to achieve success in this environment. The second critical skill identified by these managers was leadership. According to president Stephen Schilling, "This skill was seen as the ability to motivate, facilitate, and inspire telecommuters as effectively as if they were traditional office workers."

Clearly, the skills of planning and leadership are elements of any managerial relationship. But what other qualities must a manager of telecommuters possess? There are a number:

- *Comfort with supervising a remote workforce.* This is a threshold issue. Many managers simply cannot overcome their perceived need to keep employees in their sight.

- *Understanding what is required of the position.* The manager must clearly know the requirements of the position and be able to quantify or measure the output expected from the position.

- *Ability to clearly articulate goals and objectives.* Off-site staff must know what is expected of them. Management must be able to outline, specifically, the expectations and job standards that the telecommuter will be expected to meet.

- *Effective interpersonal communication.* Communication is key to a successful working relationship when manager and employees are in different physical locations. Managers must establish means of interacting with their remote staff, and allowing these staff members to interact with the rest of the staff through both face-to-face and technological methods.

- *Ability to provide clear and consistent feedback.* Managers must be willing and able to provide off-site staff with frequent and specific feedback. At any sign that the relationship is not working, or that objectives are not being met, the manager must immediately address the situation and, if necessary, rethink the approach.

To gauge managers' readiness to supervise off-site staff, Sprint offered a short assessment tool that, according to Alan Coleman, provided a useful resource both for the company and for managers. It allowed them to identify areas where improvements were needed and to indicate clearly what the expectations of this role were.

The tool consisted of two parts — seven questions on the first part assessed the manager's general management skills; nine questions on the second part assessed, specifically, the skills the manager had that would be applicable to managing remote staff. Questions consisted of true/false statements such as "I usually hold a staff meeting with all employees two times a month or less," "I rely on voicemail and email to consult with my employees," and "I regularly hold impromptu meetings." Managers rated each statement on a scale of 1 to 6, on which 1 is "not at all true" and 6 is "completely true." Managers whose responses were all 5 or higher fell into the group that was seen as having high potential to manage telecommuters. Those who scored in the 3 to 4

Not all managers are able to do away with visual supervision as a management technique. Alan Coleman of Sprint predicted that the structure of management will change as technology becomes more prevalent.

range had potential but needed to make some minor adjustments in their management style. A tool such as this one may make a world of difference in your telecommuting program, especially during the start-up and/or transition stages.

As we have seen, the skills required to manage off-site staff are comparable to the skills required when supervising any employees. Yet managers of remote workers need to fine-tune, and perhaps at times rethink, their managerial approaches.

3. Setting Objectives

Employee performance, whether employees are on- or off-site, should be measured on the attainment of established goals, and this affects a manager's approach to setting objectives.

Tom Joseph owns Bookminders, Inc., a business that provides accounting services to clients through a network of employees who work in various geographic locations — out of their homes. He says that "developing a results-oriented system for managing performance is fundamental to successful supervision of a home worker." Each employee's assignments are designed to focus on deliverables. Customers, he says, "are the most important source for determining quality." Therefore, customer satisfaction is monitored regularly through reviews that provide objective insight into both individual and company performance. In addition, Bookminders has invested in software systems that allow employees to track their time and monitor their productivity. Each month this information is gathered electronically for all employees and "analyzed to help us spot situations where training or changes to our systems will improve the overall quality of our service."

Managers must set and articulate clear goals, making sure that both they and their employees understand what is expected. In addition, more frequent evaluation may be necessary where performance, goals, and expectations can be discussed along with a thorough evaluation of any signs of problems or emerging issues.

Stephen Schilling of TCS emphasizes the need for specificity of performance objectives. "Break up the objectives into manageable chunks," he advises, "and be sure to negotiate time frames for completion of each project when applicable. Before you can review objectives, they should be clearly defined, with measurable output such as completed reports or written codes. These can be measured in quantity, quality, and time-to-complete."

You can assume almost nothing. You have to be very clear and concise in what you ask for. The process for setting objectives can be broken down into two distinct and very important areas of consideration: establishing job standards and establishing goals.

3.1 Establishing job standards

Establishing job standards is a process that begins the moment an employee — on-site or remote — is hired and continues throughout the employment relationship. It involves clear communication of expectations and standards and development of specific, measurable goals.

To develop job standards, identify the most important areas of responsibility for the position. Next, develop measurable standards for those areas.

The job description is a good starting point for indicating what is expected, but it is just a starting point. An explanation of job standards can help indicate to employees the specific expectations for their positions. Employees also need to know the goals of their positions and how those goals tie into department and company performance.

The first step in developing job standards is to identify the critical aspects of the job. What elements of the position are necessary to keep the department and the company operating efficiently? Once the areas of responsibility have been identified, three or four standards (or key results) that represent satisfactory performance levels need to be established. It is critical that these standards be objective measures of performance. More specifically, managers can use the following measures in establishing standards:

- *Quality.* How many errors, omissions, or complaints will you tolerate over a given period of time?

- *Quantity.* How many units of production will you expect over a given period of time?

- *Timeliness.* Time standards can be written in terms of daily, weekly, monthly, or quarterly deadlines for task completion or amount of turnaround time permitted.

- *Cost efficiency.* Some positions have responsibility for meeting budgets or impacting costs. In these cases your standards might reflect a maximum dollar budget or a plus or minus variance from the stated budget.

Unfortunately, not all job tasks readily lend themselves to establishing clearly defined standards. It can be challenging to come up with quantifiable measurements for certain tasks. Your goal should be to define the most critical elements of the job and, at a minimum, to establish standards that are clear enough that you have an objective way of evaluating employee performance. See Table 5 for an example of these identified goals.

TABLE 5
EXAMPLE OF GOALS OUTLINED FOR TELECOMMUTING EMPLOYEES

JOB	TASK	STANDARD
Salesperson	Generating leads	X leads/day, week, month, etc.
	Selling products	$X/week, month, quarter, year, etc.
Accountant	Creating reports	Identify specific reports that are to be made available by a certain date each month, quarter, year, etc. A standard might also be developed relating to accuracy of the reports.
Computer programmer	Program development	Specify time frame from consultation to implementation based on various common programming tasks required by the organization.

3.2 Establishing goals

Well-defined goals allow both the telecommuter and manager to have a clear understanding of expectations and provide a benchmark against which to judge performance.

Goals should be —

- Specific. A goal should state "Increase sales by 20 percent," rather than simply "Increase sales."

- Mutually agreed upon.

- Difficult, yet achievable.

- Comprehensive. Goals should cover all critical areas of the telecommuter's job.

Establishing the details of goals and objectives should be the joint responsibility of the manager and his/her employees. Together, they should cover the following tasks:

(a) Identify objectives based on organizational and departmental goals. If a system of measurement is already in place, it should work just as well in a remote working relationship as it does in the office.

(b) Develop schedules with assigned responsibility for specific task completion. Make it very clear who will be responsible for what and when deliverables are expected. Be sure that employees know how their performance is being measured and what the standards for performance are.

(c) Set up times to determine the progress of the employees' tasks. This may be a designated point during the program, upon completion of certain tasks, or on a recurring (i.e., weekly) basis.

(d) Establish ongoing means of communicating work expectations, including due dates, quality expectations, and any other measurable criteria. This may include face-to-face meetings, electronic submission of reports, or conference calls.

It is important that the manager take the time to become familiar with employees' work responsibilities and tasks. Managers must understand the time involved for completing tasks and the resources required to see projects through to completion. They must ensure that goals for off-site staff are neither more nor less stringent than those set for employees doing similar work at the office. They must establish a smoothly functioning working relationship with off-site employees, and above all, they must communicate every last detail, in detail.

Some of these details will inevitably have to be worked out along the way, as individual employees, with their specific needs and situations, settle into a work routine. However, some basic considerations can be dealt with from the start. Managers should consider the following:

• Are there core hours during which you want employees to be available?

• Are work hours flexible?

• How often should employees call the office or check their voice mail and email?

• How quickly should employees return messages?

• How often should employees communicate with their clients and coworkers?

• What security or confidentiality issues may be involved?

At Bookminders, Tom Joseph has established a quantitative system that he uses both to evaluate and to compensate his telecommuting staff. With a background in engineering, quantifying the process came naturally to him. Clients are billed based on deliverables, such as the number of journal entries made or the number of checks cut. "We bill

Don't restrict performance evaluations to an annual event. Evaluations should be a continuous process.

our clients based on a formula and we compensate our people based on that same formula," Joseph says. "Neither I nor the client have to worry about how many hours people work." In fact, Joseph believes that "the idea of setting up a deliverables-based compensation system is really the secret to what we're doing — it's what has enabled us to grow from 1 employee to 40 and to have 200 clients." Can this same process work in other organizations? Joseph thinks so. "If people could come up with a value for being able to program a certain function, or number of screens, or whatever, they could bid this work out on a per-screen or per-report basis. Telemarketers could be paid by number of calls."

4. Providing Feedback

"How am I doing?"

It is no use having established objectives if employees do not know whether they are adequately meeting them. Since remote employees are away from the office and not part of the informal communication and feedback process that often takes place between managers and employees, it is important to establish formal channels and processes for providing feedback on performance.

Start from the premise that your employees want to do a good job. Their goal is to succeed. In order to do that, they need to receive regular and specific feedback from you about how they are doing. If you are remiss in letting them know when they have or have not met or exceeded your expectations, they cannot possibly improve their performance.

Establish a regular schedule for review and feedback. Evaluation should be directly tied to the job standards and goals that you have already established with the telecommuter. When creating your review schedule, ensure that:

- Employees understand the process that will be used to review their performance. Explain how the review process will work, what criteria they will be measured on, and how frequently you will communicate with them about their performance.

- Feedback is provided regularly throughout the year — not just at the formal annual review.

- You are constructively candid. Be direct, but make sure that your constructive feedback is focused on objective job criteria, not personal characteristics or traits of the employee.

- Feedback is two-way. To maximize your relationship with your telecommuting staff, you will need feedback from them as well.

- The time you're able to spend with your remote employee may be limited, so be sure to make the most of it. Reinforce positive behaviors and respond to unsatisfactory performance immediately.

Take advantage of all communication tools available to you to provide employees with timely and ongoing feedback.

5. Communication

Communication is of the utmost importance in any employee-manager relationship, but particularly with off-site staff. It is key to success. This cannot be stressed enough.

Don't assume that all off-site staff communicate the same way. You should be flexible enough to adjust to the communication needs of each staff member.

Putting efficient communication systems in place is your first major step as a manager of off-site staff, but it doesn't end there. The system must be easy to use, probably modified for certain individual employee needs, and continually updated and improved as problems or new strategies arise. Both employee and manager must be vigilant in their adherence to the systems of communication.

In Canada, KPMG surveyed 1,600 large- and medium-sized companies in the private sector and 425 organizations in the public sector. The survey showed that a wide range of tactics were used in order to retain a sense of community between the organization and the remote worker. Ninety-one percent of employers required off-site staff to come into the office weekly or on demand. Email, teleconferencing, and written materials are also employed to keep off-site employees connected with the on-site staff and current on organization issues. In addition to standard office equipment, the majority of employers supplied communication devices such as cell phones, pagers, telephones, and modems.

To be most effective at communicating with remote workers find out the communication preferences of each of your staff members and be flexible in your interactions with them. Using only one system or schedule will not be an effective communication approach. Your goal is to develop interactions that work most effectively for all involved, and to ensure that all employees can meet their goals and be productive.

5.1 The technology of communication

"Today, collaboration is the cornerstone of business," says Jim Miller, general manager of us West Extended Workplace Solutions. "From my experience as both a remote team member and a team leader, technology can create the collaborative virtual space, but it takes more than high-tech tools to create an effective collaborative environment. It takes new ways of working with each other and using the appropriate technology tools to be able to communicate and let the distance disappear."

Miller says that the right technology tools can keep team members productive wherever their work takes them. His team uses —

(a) Collaboration software tools, such as NetMeeting. "This enables us to share (and even co-author) documents, thus reducing the number of drafts that we need to fax or email and maintaining version control."

(b) Speakerphones. "But only," he says, "if we don't sound like we're speaking from a cave." Miller recommends investing in good-quality speakerphones or, even better, headsets.

(c) A team "white space." "We have a place on our intranet where my team can post messages, documents, calendars, databases, and any frequently requested information such as lists, presentations, or even recommendations on hotels for the road warriors."

(d) Voice or video conferencing tools. "Sometimes we use the simple three-way calling feature and other times we use a voice conference bridge. We've even used video conferencing to review rough cuts of a video." The most cost-effective options, Miller says, "will vary depending on the number of participants and the goals of your virtual meeting."

Technology can help to maintain communication with distant team members, but, Miller advises, it's important to establish some guidelines and rules. For example:

(a) Be prepared. It's a waste of your teammates' time if you haven't looked at the agenda, read the materials, and thought about the topic at hand before the virtual meeting. Ask to reschedule if necessary.

(b) Make your presence known. If a person new to the group joins a call, then throughout the duration of the meeting, everyone should identify himself or herself before speaking. If you must join the call late, announce your presence — no lurking!

(c) Keep extraneous noise to a minimum. Shuffling papers and side conversations are distracting and can even drown the main thread of conversation. (One way to control noise is to use the mute button until you speak.)

(d) Do not multi-task. For a set period of time, devote your full attention to the team. Believe me, they can tell if you don't!

(e) Avoid "stepping on someone's line." Actors learn not to talk on top of each other so everyone can be heard. The same rule applies to conference calls.

(f) Use active listening skills. If you're in a voice conference, you do not have the advantage of "listening" to body language, and need to try harder to fully hear what the person may or may not be saying. Use rephrasing techniques to be sure, instead of assuming.

(g) Encourage participation. If you're the team leader, make sure all team members voice their opinions. The shy ones may need extra time and encouragement to participate.

Stephen Schilling of TeleCommute Solutions offers the following tips to enhance virtual communication:

- Establish regular, mutually agreed-upon communication times. Telephone calls, teleconferences, videoconferences, and chat areas can all be entered at an agreed-upon time.

- Make certain that off-site workers understand their worth to the organization. Devise methods to make these workers feel included in the team spirit. For example, have good-natured team contests or virtual coffee breaks.

- Have social events periodically where all workers can meet in person.

- Circulate an online newsletter to keep everyone abreast of projects, discoveries, innovations, and even errors. Solicit contributions from all team members.

- If your workers are regionalized, appoint one of the workers to be the initiator of communication and social activities. Groups that meet informally to share values or special interests can be effective.

- If in-person meetings are out of the question at a particular time, do your best to hold a videoconference. Visual communication enhances verbal communication.

- If team members are within convenient driving (or flying) distance, it's still a great idea to have weekly meetings at most or monthly meetings at least. There is no replacement for in-person sessions. Team meetings might also be held in various home-office environments to legitimize the workplace of the telecommuter.

- If workers are job sharing, have a formal handoff procedure, as well as the technology for informal communication for special situations and questions.

- Constantly research and implement state-of-the-art technology for (maintaining) productive communication.

6. Maintaining Involvement

One of the greatest fears that remote staff have is that they will become invisible. They worry about being out of touch and overlooked for key assignments and promotions. As a manager, you should be aware of this concern and take steps to ensure that your remote workers maintain their involvement and visibility within the organization. There are a number of ways in which you can do this:

- Be honest about the changes that will occur when an employee is working off-site. Obviously, relationships will change. Address the issue head on and help the employee work through his or her concerns.

- Emphasize to the remote employee the role that he or she plays in maintaining visibility. Encourage off-site staff to take advantage of all communication tools available to them and stress the importance of establishing frequent and effective communication links to the head office.

- Provide support staff and other staff members with the home phone numbers and email addresses of off-site staff members so they won't be left out of general office communications.

- Keep in touch with off-site staff and provide frequent updates about what's happening back at the head office. Consider email newsletters that can provide regular reports on news and events.

- Don't overlook off-site employees when selecting members for team projects, tasks, or promotions.

- Schedule regular and frequent trips to the office so off-site employees have the opportunity to interact with other members of the staff.

- Include team-building activities at regular meetings.

- Schedule frequent evaluation sessions.

- Be flexible and willing to change your style of communication or consider unique modes of interaction based on the needs of individual employees.

- Make sure that off-site staff are offered the same professional growth opportunities as the rest of the staff. Some ways of doing this might include:
  - Allowing off-site staff to join professional organiztions related to their current jobs or jobs they are interested in.
  - Sending off-site staff to courses to enhance their skills or help them develop additional skills.
  - Working with off-site staff on career advancement within the organization.
  - Recommending off-site staff for task forces and committees.

In a study conducted by the Georgetown University School of Business for Bell Atlantic, telecommuters at several companies — including American Express, Marriott International, and Fannie Mae — were interviewed over a period of several months. Common disadvantages that were pointed out included the fear of being left out of communication, the manager being difficult to reach when the telecommuter had a problem, and the available technologies not being compatible with their needs.

Companies have found ways to address the common pitfalls of managing remote workers, however. American Express, for example, assigns off-site staff a "buddy" in the home office to be sure they are informed. Off-site employees are encouraged to spend time during work hours talking with their buddies about work-related issues to keep abreast of office developments and boost morale. Recommendations based on the Georgetown survey included training and improved communication, which have been discussed at length, and also a redefinition of authority. The survey suggests that successful off-site relationships demand that workers move away from the traditional management paradigm towards a more interdependent balance of power.

7. Motivating Off-site Staff

The strategies and techniques necessary to motivate off-site staff are the same as those you should already be using with your on-site employees. The following are some strategies that will work with employees both on-site and off-site:

- *Listen to your off-site staff members' concerns.* Make sure that you are sincere in listening to your employees and that you give fair and honest consideration to their questions and concerns.

If the off-site arrangement isn't working out, take action as soon as possible. Ignoring minor problems will lead to major problems in the future.

- *Be available.* Make sure that your off-site employees have ready access to you by phone, email, or in person.

- *Share information.* Off-site employees have a heightened need to feel included. When you share information with them, they will feel more involved in what's happening at the company. This can be as simple as letting them know about an employee's going-away party or as involved as reviewing information about the organization's strategic plan.

- *Give ample recognition for a job well done.* Provide off-site staff with frequent feedback about how they're doing and make sure that you share their accomplishments and achievements with on-site staff.

- *Provide opportunities for professional growth.* As previously discussed, remote employees, like any employees, need to be motivated by the opportunity for growth.

- *Treat all employees as individuals.* It is rare to find two individuals who have the same skills or personal objectives. While one off-site employee may react favorably to infrequent contact and open-ended expectations, another may require frequent visits to the office and very clear and specific direction. Take the time to get to know your off-site staff members and to understand their individual goals and objectives.

- *Be open to new ideas.* Employee feedback is important to any company's success. Listen carefully to every idea presented and give each fair consideration. If you decide to use an idea, make sure that you give credit to the individual who made the suggestion.

- *Have fun!* All work and no play can make all of us dull. When employees have been working nonstop for a period of time, they need and appreciate a little time off. Allow some breaks and take time to celebrate successes. There are many ways to show your appreciation to employees. Be creative.

8. If the Relationship Doesn't Work

Not every alternative work relationship will be a successful one. Sometimes off-site employees decide that they miss the interaction and security of the traditional office setting. Or you may decide that productivity or service to customers is suffering from the alternative work arrangement. In either case, it is important to act quickly to remedy the situation.

Unresolved issues can have a negative impact in a number of ways. There may be direct monetary costs to the organization. There may be productivity costs. There will almost certainly be morale problems, especially if you fail to take action. Other employees will quickly become frustrated if remote workers are not pulling their weight.

A common mistake made by managers is to wait to see if the issue will resolve itself. Few people welcome conflict, and — at least initially — it appears far easier to avoid conflict than to confront it. In fact, avoiding a problem may actually result in greater frustration, effort, and cost to the organization at a later date.

If a problem surfaces, address it immediately. Just as when addressing performance issues with on-site employees, your feedback should be immediate, predictable, impersonal, and consistent. Approach the employee as soon as the issue has been noticed or reported. Selecting the appropriate tool to communicate with the employee is very important. While a minor issue (a reminder to turn in a report, for example) may be handled via email, other more critical issues (i.e., a customer complaint about lack of availability) may require a face-to-face meeting. Make sure that you don't use technology as a means of avoiding an uncomfortable situation.

Your comments should remain focused on the task and the objective measures of performance you have established, not on the personal habits or characteristics of the employee. Do not criticize a remote worker for something that an employee in a comparable position at the workplace would not be criticized for. The agreement you created at the beginning of the relationship can provide a good frame of reference and guide for addressing problems in the relationship (see Chapter 3).

Finally, don't treat the employee as an adversary. Address the issue without lecturing, nagging, or losing your temper. Make sure to allow the employee an opportunity to tell his or her side of the story, and be sure to listen with an open mind.

If a problem arises, you will have to discuss the situation with the off-site employee. During this discussion, you should —

- have notes and make use of them,

- explain the facts as completely as possible,

- ask the employee for his or her perspective,

- expect and allow some emotional venting,

- be specific about the consequences of continued problems, and

- provide a system for follow-up.

One of the most pervasive problems that managers have — whether managing on-site or off-site staff — is failure to document thoroughly. Be meticulous in your documentation.

If the situation progresses or becomes worse, it may be necessary to either terminate the alternative work arrangement or terminate the employment relationship. In either case, it is important that you have documented the issues that have led to your decision and that you address the problem immediately and objectively.

When a performance-related incident occurs, record the date it happened, what specifically occurred, and the interaction you had with the employee. Make certain that you have informed the employee of each infraction that occurred and that you have clearly indicated what would happen if future occurrences took place.

Your goal in dealing with performance issues is not to move quickly to terminate the work arrangement or employment relationship, but to maintain a productive and effective employee. In providing the employee with information about behaviors or actions that are inconsistent with policy or expectations, you should also provide coaching and assistance in improving employee behavior. Perhaps more training is required. Perhaps the tools available to the employee are insufficient to perform the job effectively. However, do not hesitate to terminate the work arrangement if it is not meeting the needs of the department or the organization.

9. Additional Tips for Managers of Off-Site Staff

The remote employee/manager relationship is an evolving one. It will be continually fine-tuned to suit the changing needs of the business, the individual needs of each employee and the professional growth of the manager. Always seek advice and examples from other managers and also from remote staff members, whether they are working for you or not.

Remember that a trusting relationship is critical. Try not to over-manage your off-site staff members, making them feel as though they are under constant surveillance. Be careful, though, to find a balance between over-managing and ignoring off-site staff. Try not to become too much of an absentee manager. Maintaining the right amount of contact with your off-site employees will allow them to feel involved without feeling stifled.

You are bound to face some challenges in your alternative work relationships, particularly if these arrangements are new to you and/or your organization. Good organization and communication skills are your best combative measures. Help your off-site staff members organize their work. Don't expect perfection, and don't expect everyone to be successful. Some employees adjust more readily to a remote working relationship than others. Working remotely may not work for everyone. When it doesn't, take immediate steps to develop a more workable solution.

See Sample 4 for more tips from AG Communication Systems, and Sample 5 for tips from the University of Texas.

10. Case Study

Best Buy Co., Inc., was established in 1966 and has grown over the years to operate a global portfolio of brands for the retail market, offering entertainment and technology solutions.

Best Buy employs about 4000 workers in its corporate headquarters. In 2003, Best Buy introduced those workers to ROWE — the "Results-Only Work Environment" (ROWE), a radical departure from traditional corporate reporting structures which involves no requirement to be physically in the office and no specific work hours. Staff are free to work when they want, where they want, as long as they get their work done. Performance, as in any good flexible work environment, is measured based on output — not hours.

A radical experiment, indeed, but one that has achieved results. Productivity has increased 35 percent, engagement has increased, and voluntary turnover has declined.

Best Buy didn't wasn't one of the early corporate adopters of flexible work schedules and it didn't invent ROWE. Two of its employees did. Cali Yost and Jody Thompson are the creators of the "Results-Only Work Environment" concept and they created it from the "ground up" as a grass-roots initiative at Best Buy. Today they've taken the show on the road, introducing ROWE to a number of other companies, developing their own website and blog, and writing the book, *Why Work Sucks and How to Fix It* (Portfolio Hardcover, 2008).

In 2001, Best Buy surveyed headquarter employees and was disturbed by the results. Employees didn't feel their managers trusted them to do their jobs and were far from satisfied with their work environment. Ressler, manager of Best Buy's work/life balance programs at the time began experimenting with various flexible work arrangements in the retail operations division. Joined by Thomson, they set up to institute change on a large scale. Discounting the alternative scheduling options already commonly in use, Ressler and Thompson chose a far more radical approach.

TELEWORKING ISSUES — AG COMMUNICATION SYSTEMS TELEWORK HANDBOOK

Before your employees begin working at home, you might keep in mind some of these issues that can be sensitive to both teleworkers and non-teleworkers.

Suggestions for Managing Non-Teleworkers in a Teleworking Environment

Selection. As you select participants in the teleworking program, you need to work carefully with non-teleworkers to avoid their feeling "left out." Prepare in advance the necessary documentation to support your decision of who was chosen to telework. Should you have non-teleworking employees who have been excluded from the program because of poor job performance, you might begin a program to assist those employees in raising their job performance level.

Team Effort. Non-teleworkers are as critical to the program's effectiveness as the teleworkers. The success of your group depends on the efforts of everyone. Understanding the components of what makes your team successful will guarantee continued success.

Team Support. Non-teleworkers shouldn't be expected to do extra work in the office while teleworkers are working at home. Try to make sure you're consistent in assigning and providing support to your employees.

Communications Links. Establish guidelines for contacting teleworkers when an issue arises in the office that requires immediate action. Don't expect non-teleworkers to work on their own assignments as well as handling problems for teleworkers. Establish guidelines for answering the teleworkers' phones while they are teleworking. Refrain from advising callers, "Bobby is at home today." Instead, say "Bobby is unavailable at this time. I'll be happy to have her return your call as soon as she is able." Or, "You can reach Bobby at (phone number)." Additionally, have teleworkers call the office at regular intervals, and provide support staff with home phone numbers.

Contingency Plans. Establish Murphy's Law strategies to guide your workgroup through "what if" situations. Address all issues that are pertinent to the team and encourage participation from the entire team.

What Happens If It's Not Working? You and your teleworkers must understand that not everyone who tries teleworking is successful. Some reasons why the teleworker may need to end his or her participation in the program are:

Uncontrollable distractions — The neighbors and family just don't understand that while the employee is at home, they are unavailable for other activities.

Cabin fever — Being at home 24 hours a day becomes unacceptable.

Productivity and quality of work — The employee's productivity and/or the quality of the employee's work has declined since the employee has been participating in the teleworking program.

Desire or need to be around people — The employee discovers that the need for social interaction is a critical factor in his or her life.

If it becomes apparent that the employee must end his or her participation in the project, don't hold a grudge against that employee because he or she was not successful in his or her efforts. Help the employee to understand that he or she is of value to the organization and bring him or her back into the office as quickly as possible.

MANAGING TELECOMMUTERS: TIPS FOR SUPERVISORS
(UNIVERSITY OF TEXAS — HOUSTON HEALTH SCIENCE CENTER)

The University of Houston's Health Science Center offers advice on managing telecommuters:

→ Managing telecommuters is not unlike managing employees on-site. It requires management skills such as goal setting, assessing progress, giving regular feedback, and managing based on outcomes. Some managers prefer dividing objectives into smaller parts and reviewing work more frequently — at least initially — to ensure the telecommuter is on track.

→ Focus on quality of work, not necessarily quantity of time spent off-site.

→ Identify and discuss problem areas as soon as possible and develop a plan of action to avoid bigger problems down the road.

→ Be flexible enough to make changes when and where necessary.

→ Include telecommuters in all appropriate office meetings, both official and social, to prevent telecommuters from feeling isolated from the office team.

→ Review sections on selecting telecommuters and creating a safe/efficient work site in the Telecommuting guide to assist in managing telecommuters in your area.

→ Remember that use of telecommuting is first and foremost a supervisor's option and should be reviewed/approved with careful consideration of the missions of your department and the University.

→ While telecommuting can sometimes look like a benefit only to employees, most studies show that, based on benefits from such things as decreased employee turnover and increased employee productivity, a company can save several thousand dollars a year per telecommuter.

→ Supervisors should give telecommuters at least 24 hours' notice if they plan to visit the alternate work site to check on University equipment, the work environment, etc.

Copyright© 1997-2001 from The University of Texas — Houston Health Science Center — www.uth.tmc.edu

With ROWE:

- There is no need for schedules
- Nobody focuses on "how many hours did you work?"
- Nobody feels overworked, stressed out, or guilty
- People at all levels stop wasting the company's time and money
- Teamwork, morale, and engagement soar
- There's no judgment on how people spend their time

Benefits that Best Buy and others have attained include: increased productivity, reduced voluntary turnover, increased engagement, and bottom line improvements. While still management-controlled, ROWE offers employees maximum flexibility to work when they want to work. The primary requirement: to meet established goals.

Of the approximately 4,000 employees at Best Buy headquarters, about 60 percent or 2,400 have converted to this new way of work.

Employees love the flexibility. As one employee said: "I like working for a company that understands life outside of work. ROWE has enabled me to probably work more hours, however, feel that I have time for everything in my life. I am therefore less stressed and can work more and more efficiently. I feel more in control of my work and that I have more to offer, which makes me feel good as a person."

ROWE employees can work not only when they want, but where they want. That can mean from home — it can mean from the corner Starbucks — it can mean from the beach. It literally doesn't matter — as long as the work gets done.

And, equally if not more important, managers are also on board. "In my 10+ years as a manager, I have never seen a concept that could more quickly or completely unleash the power of employees to focus on customers' needs, eliminate waste, motivate teams, or attract and retain talent better than ROWE," said one manager. "It is an essential tool for managers to be successful and for companies to remain competitive in today's business environment and it is the one tool I never want to be without."

Chapter 8
PROGRAM OUTCOMES

"It is important to learn from the research and be informed of the consequences telecommuting might have — both positive and negative — on the organization and on the employees."

— Theresa Pitman
President, Pitman Technology Group Inc.

Executive Summary

How will I know if the program is successful?

That's really up to you. Developing some process for measuring the effectiveness of your efforts to allow employees to work in flexible, off-site settings is essential. In fact, you may have several different types of measurements in place, depending on the type and number of alternative work relationships your organization has. Measurement should be based on the objectives you establish for the program and may incorporate both qualitative and quantitative measures. For instance, you may rely on verbal reports from off-site employees and their managers, surveys, or quantitative productivity measures.

What if the program is operating according to the company guidelines, but is still not working?

If your program is still relatively new, you may have to accommodate a learning-curve period. But this is a time for revision and fine tuning. Collect whatever results are available, and discuss methods of improvement with off-site employees, telecommuters, their managers, and other staff.

Why do telecommuting programs fail?

There are a variety of reasons why telecommuting programs fail. Chief among these, however, are poorly defined objectives (not knowing what you wanted to achieve from the program in the first place), selecting the wrong individual or the wrong job for telecommuting, poorly conceived or nonexistent guidelines, and lack of communication.

PROGRAM OUTCOMES

Properly implemented and conscientiously managed, your alternative work arrangements should prove highly beneficial to both your company and your employees. When the operation is running smoothly, workers should be more productive, overhead costs should be reduced, and employee retention should show improvement. The overall success (or failure) of the program should be as rigorously monitored as the fine details of its operations.

1. Measuring Program Outcomes

Its important to establish methods of evaluating the effectiveness of any alternative work arrangements as well as the morale of both off- and on-site staff. This can be done by measuring output, by surveying those involved in the program, and through direct observation. Technology also affords the means to evaluate program outcomes by measuring how many employees use remote access, for instance; or by keeping track of how long online sessions last, when employees are logging in, and how frequently they connect.

The process of evaluating performance should be built in from the outset. Both qualitative and quantitative information can be used for assessment. The criteria you select for assessment should be based on

The overall success (or failure) of the program should be as rigorously monitored as the fine details of its operations.

the objectives you initially established. For example, if your primary objective for allowing for flexible work arrangements was to improve employee morale and reduce turnover, you might include a qualitative measurement of morale, perhaps self-reports from off-site employees and other staff members, as well as quantitative measures of turnover. If your primary objective was to reduce office space costs, again, you should be able to apply quantitative measures of costs based on a before-and-after comparison.

Depending on your objectives and the measures of success you've selected, there are a variety of sources from which to obtain information. These sources may include individuals, for instance, off-site staff members, their managers, on-site employees, and customers. Sources may also include data, such as turnover data, office-supply expense data, and productivity records.

Feedback to the participants in the program is very important. Share the results of whatever you're measuring and involve off-site staff (and their on-site colleagues) in any discussions on how to improve results.

2. Why Alternative Work Arrangements Fail

Do flexible work arrangements programs really deliver the results that companies expect? According to Marc J. Wallace, Jr., PhD, a founding partner of the Center for Workplace Effectiveness, Inc., in Northbrook, Illinois, and co-author of *Work & Rewards in the Virtual Workplace: A New Deal for Organizations & Employees* (AMACOM, 1998): no.

"Our research experience has been that telecommuting, so far, has been a disappointment for most organizations that have tried it," says Wallace. He points to four major downfalls, or problem areas, that tend to emerge over time:

(1) Lack of quality face time with people, particularly where high interaction is required by the work process or the nature of the work itself. When an employee is attached by the umbilical cord of the modem or other electronic medium, he or she does not have the full advantage of body language, of multiple channels of communication, and the very real, but difficult to measure, intangible of human interaction.

(2) Absence from the workplace. Unless your remote employees are extremely sophisticated in terms of coordinating, handing things off, and leaving instructions, it can lead to a less — rather than more — productive environment.

(3) Lost creativity. The inventiveness and energy behind innovation can get lost when people aren't interacting with each other on a regular basis. A lot of things that were good ideas get lost and are never brought to fruition because there isn't this opportunity that often presents itself in working teams to get creative and to brainstorm.

(4) Unmet expectations. There is an assumption in telecommuting that, somehow, home is going to be a friendly, easier, quieter place to work than the office. The normal life that goes on at home can become more of a distraction — not less of a distraction.

"These points," Wallace says, "should be the basis of any alternative work arrangement. I believe that it's necessary, if one is going to institute alternative work options, that one takes those four circumstances into account and train for them."

As we have seen in this book, there are a number of reasons why these relationships may fail; but we have also seen that with appropriate methods of program implementation and management, there are many more reasons why such relationships should succeed.

In "Moving Telecommuting Forward: An Examination of Organizational Variables," a report based on research conducted at the National Center for Transportation and Industrial Productivity at the New Jersey Institute of Technology (NJIT), a number of recommendations were made to improve the effectiveness of telecommuting, including the following:

(a) *Readiness.* To assess the readiness of your organization for telecommuting, conduct an audit to find out how much casual telecommuting already exists. Your organization may be further ahead than you think.

(b) *Communication.* Assess the extent to which your organization is using email, phone conferences, and other asynchronous forms of communication. The greater variety in telecommunication modalities used, the more readily the organization can adapt to telecommuting.

(c) *Management.* Part-time telecommuting does not appear to require much change in management style or process. Reassure managers regarding the limited requirements for change. The fact that these managers perceived virtually no change in their behaviors toward part-time telecommuters in comparison to non-telecommuters suggests that future studies should focus on full-time telecommuting arrangements. This project will continue to add managers to the database already developed.

(d) *Learning Curve.* Where full-time telecommuting is contemplated, managers and employees need to go through a learning curve as they adjust to a new working arrangement. Both should be prepared to give added effort in communication while the manager adapts to not having the employee readily available. Both need to go through some orientation to telecommuting issues. There are several sources and websites that are helpful in giving guidelines for successful telecommuting programs.

(e) *Equity.* The problem here involves opportunities for promotion while telecommuting full-time for an extended duration. While there may be some positions available, in most large organizations this currently does not seem to be a viable alternative. Career counseling should alert employees to maintain visibility. If long-term, full-time telecommuting is a job requirement for an employee, the employee needs to be counseled about ramifications for career progress. One alternative is to seek an organization that is comfortable with telecommuting as a full-time work arrangement. As an example, the CEO of one of the organizations sampled liked telecommuting. Such an organization would accommodate someone who has needs for long-term, full-time telecommuting.

(f) *Selection.* Currently, telecommuting is available at a professional level in the organizations sampled, but not to hourly workers. Those wishing to telecommute can select it as an option, but most organizations are not promoting it. This lack of promotion may give the impression that it is a second-class work arrangement. If an organization gives the option, then it should publicize the option as an alternative work arrangement through its Human Resources department or equivalent.

(g) *Teamwork.* This way of assigning tasks is disrupted less by telecommuting than one might think. Teamwork while telecommuting places a priority on organizational skills and attention to detail so that participants in teleconferences have available all materials that one would normally have available at a meeting. With email and fax, this should present little difficulty beyond that of getting material out before the meeting begins (as opposed to bringing material to a meeting). Coordination for a teleconference requires efforts similar to coordinating times for a face-to-face meeting. The additional element to deal with is the technology of the phone conference. Communication in between can be handled by email. With distribution lists, email is often a better manager of communication than the team leader, who may forget to relay messages to everyone, may relay incomplete messages, or may distort or delay relaying messages.

(h) *Moving toward remote management.* An interesting and unexpected trend discerned in this project is the move toward remote management regardless of whether employees are telecommuting or not. That is, work is becoming distributed over wider geographical areas, and managers are more and more likely to be based at locations that are apart from their subordinates. This portends a change so that managers, in general, will need the same skill set and style found among managers of telecommuters. These skills place a priority on organization, communication over a variety of modalities, an ability to set specific and unambiguous goals with employees, and the capacity to build trust of subordinates based on their performance.

Creating successful work relationships with off-site staff requires careful attention to detail, flexibility in responding to unique personal and departmental needs, clear objectives, and identified methods of monitoring and measuring the success of alternative work arrangements. The specifics of each situation will vary by company and by position, but these general needs remain consistent across all programs.

Jim Miller of US West Extended Workplace Solutions advises companies to decide exactly what they hope to gain from a telecommuting program before trying to settle the minor details.

3. Case Study

Pitney Bowes is a Fortune 500 company headquartered in Southwestern, Connecticut. A mainstream technology company, Pitney Bowes was founded in 1920 and has $6.4 billion in revenue, more than 35,000 employees, and does business in 130 countries. A long-standing recognized leader in commuter services and traffic reduction, particularly near the company's headquarters in Stamford and throughout Connecticut, Pitney Bowes offers a number of unique commuting options and services for employees, including a free shuttle service for employees between its facilities and the Stamford MetroNorth train station that has been in place for approximately 12 years. Pitney Bowes also offers its employees flexible work arrangements, including telecommuting, and has been doing so for a number of years.

Flexibility for staff has been championed, to a large degree, by Pitney Bowes director of workforce effectiveness, Ed Houghton, who takes advantage of these flexible options himself. Houghton has actively promoted traffic reduction programs, flexibility, and corporate responsibility throughout the region at local chambers of commerce and business council meetings and at several national conferences. Houghton works a four-day compressed work week, an option he says that has helped him delay retirement and retain the balance he was seeking between work and family life.

While Pitney Bowes has been offering these options since long before recent concerns over skyrocketing gas costs, Houghton says that the amount of interest shown by employees is definitely on the rise.

Pitney Bowes employees work in a wide range of formal and informal flexible work arrangements. These arrangements vary in availability and scope based primarily on business need. Examples of the types of flexible arrangements offered and supported include:

- Flextime

- Staggered hours

- Summer hours

- Compressed work weeks (four days a week, ten hours a day, and nine days every two weeks, roughly nine hours a day)

- Telecommuting/teleworking

A Flexible Work Arrangement page on the company's intranet site offers information, tools, and success stories for employees and managers interested in flex options. While policies have been in place for a number of years, the intranet site now makes information about the program options readily available to staff throughout the organization.

Information available includes specific, very helpful, instructions for employees on how to present a request for an alternative work arrangement most effectively, with a clear focus on the business case for such arrangements.

In addition to the flexible options mentioned above, Pitney Bowes also offers hoteling capabilities at its largest facilities. Visitor centers are available to employees and visitors at select Pitney Bowes locations as a convenient option for getting work done from a variety of locations. Almost all are equipped with phone and computer connections, faxes, printers, and copiers. A significant number of employees regularly work at facilities closer to their homes on heavy traffic days, and use the visitor centers. Many employees have soft phones providing direct connection to their office phone through a laptop.

Pitney Bowes has been recognized for its efforts through a variety of awards and recognitions including recognition in 2007 by the US EPA as one of the Best Workplaces for Commuters, a national list featuring employers that offer their employees superior commuter benefits.

Appendix 1
TELECOMMUTING PROPOSAL

Sample Telecommuting Proposal
The University of Texas — Houston Health Science Center (www.uth.tmc.edu)

Date:

Employee's Name:

Supervisor's Name:

I, _____ (name), am requesting to
telecommute with my job as _____ (job title), beginning on
_____ (date).

Potential impact of my telecommuting on my department may include the following (e.g., impact on operations/work flow, potential advantages, potential disadvantages):

_____

_____

_____

The schedule I would desire for telecommuting is:

_____

_____

_____

My alternative work site would be:

_____

A description of this work site is:

_____

(e.g., a spare bedroom with door away from most family activity that is well ventilated, has good lighting, many electrical outlets, phone jack, etc.)

Equipment I would need from this department would include:

_____

Equipment I already own and am willing to use includes:

_____

My expectations from the department to support me in telecommuting are:

_____

(e.g., provide 486 PC, fax, modem, telephone line, pay for insurance on equipment)

My expectations for supervision are:

_____

(e.g., frequency, how work would be reviewed)

Check one:

☐   I do not have dependent care needs

☐   I do have dependent care needs that are met as follows:

_____

_____

_____

I would like to review my telecommuting agreement in _____ months to determine its effectiveness on my job performance.

Thank you for your consideration.

_____

Employee Name

Appendix 2
TELECOMMUTING POLICY
AG Communication Systems Sample

Telecommuting Policy 1

1.0 Policy

Employees who work away from AGCS and connect via telephone or computer connections are defined as teleworkers. AGCS supports teleworking as an alternative work arrangement shifting the location of work away from the main offices of AGCS and to the worker. Coaches/Managers are encouraged to give employees' teleworking requests every consideration. Teleworking and teleworkers are classified and supported dependent upon the level and frequency of teleworking to include casual, part-time, job demand, full-time, and mobile, as well as teleworkers at satellite offices.

2.0 Scope

This Policy applies to regular full-time and part-time non-union salaried employees at all AGCS locations, and provides guidelines to employees working away from the primary workplace. Where state or local laws contain mandatory requirements that differ from the provisions of this policy, such legal requirements prevail for employees working in affected locations.

3.0 Purpose

To provide another tool for flexible work alternatives to better meet the needs of the company, management, and employees of AGCS as well as the environmental concerns of the communities in which we do business.

AGCS anticipates teleworking to benefit AGCS, employees, and the community by:

➤ better meeting both business and employee needs

➤ attracting and retaining a diverse and talented workforce

➤ helping the environment by achieving trip reduction goals as well as decreasing traffic

➤ congestion and vehicle emissions to reduce air pollution in all of our business communities

4.0 Definitions

4.1 Casual Teleworker — The casual teleworker has a dedicated office at AGCS and occasionally takes work home. The work completed away from the office may be in addition to the normal work day as assigned, unassigned, or casual overtime or it may be a day selected by the employee based on a management approved teleworking agreement.

4.2 Part-time Teleworker — The part-time teleworker has a dedicated office at AGCS and works from home based upon a management approved teleworking agreement on a routine schedule of 1 or 2 days per week or regularly works overtime at home for a specified period of time.

4.3 Job Demand Teleworker — The job demand teleworker has a dedicated office at AGCS and is required by his or her job situation to work 8 or more non-prime shift hours per week at home.

4.4 Full-time Teleworker — The full-time teleworker does not have an assigned office at AGCS and works primarily from home based upon a management approved teleworking agreement. The full-time teleworker may reserve and use a hoteling office, if available, during periods of work spent at the main offices of AGCS.

4.5 Mobile Teleworker — The mobile teleworker has a dedicated office at AGCS, however he or she has the need to travel on a regular basis and conduct business from a variety of locations using a telephone and/or personal computer and connecting to AGCS systems remotely.

4.6 Satellite Office — Based upon business needs, AGCS may establish satellite offices in other cities convenient to the customer or in areas closer to an available workforce. Marketing sales offices, construction field offices, or neighborhood offices would be defined as satellite offices.

4.7 Hoteling — An unassigned office which is shared by others and is equipped with a workstation and telephone. This office can be reserved by a dedicated teleworker for one or two days while attending to business at the offices of AGCS.

4.8 Teleworking Category Matrix — The level and type of support provided for each type of teleworker is shown on the Teleworking Category Matrix attached to this policy.

5.0 Responsibilities

5.1 Employee responsibilities:

➤ Become familiar with the Policy and Guidelines for Teleworking, the Teleworking Agreement, and related documents within the *Teleworking Handbook*. The formal Teleworking Agreement is required for all but mobile types of teleworking arrangements.

➤ Except for those in the casual and mobile categories, potential teleworkers need to complete the Telework Feasibility Survey form, supplied as a part of the *Teleworking Handbook*, to determine if the job and the individual are suited for teleworking.

➤ Propose the teleworking arrangement to the coach or manager for approval, review with the team if applicable. If the schedule and proposal are acceptable to both, complete and sign the Teleworking Agreement form and return it to the coach/manager and together review it with HR and its Teleworking Facilitator.

➤ Become familiar with the Safety and Ergonomic Guidelines in the Teleworking Handbook. Use these guidelines to set up a dedicated work area at home (or other management approved place) that is safe for the employee and others entering it.

➤ Establish work practices that make teleworking productive for the company and transparent to customers.

➤ Abide by the terms and conditions of the Teleworking Agreement and teleworking guidelines.

➤ Report to the office as required for work, meetings, and training at the request of management or customers.

➤ Safeguard proprietary information and all AGCS assets, including company data in keeping with all AGCS security and computer usage policies and those contained in sections 11.0 and 12.0 of this policy. Failure to comply with these policies will result in loss of teleworking privileges.

➤ Determine federal, state, and local tax implications resulting from teleworking and satisfy such at their own expense, along with their other personal tax obligations.

➤ Consult with Safety and Health in setting up an office design.

➤ Set up work area at home.

➤ Comply with applicable state and local zoning ordinances.

➤ Comply with all other terms and conditions of employment.

5.2 Team responsibilities:

➤ Input to the Telework Feasibility survey, inputting information to assist in the evaluation of the feasibility of teleworking.

➤ Develop team guidelines on how the team and the teleworker will work together to on a day to day basis, complete projects, and maintain customer satisfaction.

➤ Communicate with teleworker on a regular basis, including meetings, normal day to day work relations. Teams should make the location of the teleworker transparent to the completion of objectives.

5.3 Coach/Manager responsibilities:

➤ Become familiar with the Policy and Guidelines for Teleworking, the Teleworking Agreement, and related documents within the *Teleworking Handbook*.

➤ Encourage and work with employee requests to telework, using the Teleworking Feasibility Survey supplied as a part of the *Teleworking Handbook*, and implement a teleworking arrangement if beneficial to AGCS business, employees, and the environment. Coach/managers are encouraged to be flexible and give teleworking requests every consideration.

➤ Make the "business decision" as to whether a request to telework meets the necessary requirements and makes sense from an AGCS perspective. This decision is based on the impact on AGCS, including productivity gains or losses, effect on customer service, employee retention, team and/or department issues and costs.

➤ Have the employee complete a Teleworking Agreement, file the original in the employee personnel files kept by the coach/manager, and retain for one year after the teleworking arrangement ends. Send a copy of the agreement to the hr Teleworking Facilitator and give the employee a copy for his or her files.

➤ Update Teleworking Agreement if any aspect of the arrangement covered by the agreement changes, obtain employee's signature, and provide copies as stated in the paragraph immediately above.

➤ Review computer security and safeguarding of proprietary information with the employee.

➤ Maintain an accurate inventory, including the location of AGCS-owned equipment taken off-site. The employee is required to fill out a High Technology Removal form (FM-44). It should be completed by management and employee when the Teleworking Agreement is finalized. File the yellow copy of FM-44 and retain it for one year after the teleworking arrangement ends.

➤ Notify Payroll if employee works from a state different than from their AGCS work location state.

➤ Continue normal management activities including performance appraisals, career development, ongoing feedback, and other normal communications.

➤ Provide support as required to meet the needs of teleworkers. Meet with the employee on a quarterly basis to assess how it is going and discuss productivity, issues, or difficulties.

5.4 HR Teleworking Facilitator responsibilities:

➤ Advise and consult with employees and coaches/managers wishing to implement a teleworking arrangement. Work with the Corporate Communications department to communicate teleworking.

➤ Provide clarification of the teleworking policy and provide advice and training on teleworking practices.

➤ Answer teleworking questions for both employee and management and provide training to the teleworker, teams, or management as required.

➤ Track the number of teleworkers and evaluate the program for effectiveness.

5.5 ITS Teleworking Facilitator responsibilities:

➤ Advise and consult with employees and coaches/managers about the technical issues associated with teleworking, including availability of computer hardware, software, and connectivity options.

➤ Coordinate its support for teleworkers.

➤ Resolve its related telework issues.

➤ Arrange for and coordinate technical training for teleworkers

5.6 Health and Safety representatives will provide consultation or training information on setting up the office using good ergonomic practices.

6.0 Compensation and Benefits

The employee's compensation, benefits, and company sponsored insurance coverage are not affected by the teleworking arrangement.

7.0 Taxes

Employees participating in the teleworking arrangement are responsible for determining federal, state, and local tax implications resulting from working at home and to satisfy each at their own expense along with other personal tax obligations. Employees should refer any tax related questions to their personal tax advisor.

8.0 Hours of Work and Overtime

An employee's standard work hours are unaffected by the teleworking arrangement. The daily schedule is specified in the Teleworking Agreement.

The AGCS Overtime policy extends to teleworking arrangements. Refer to HR policy 108, Overtime Compensation, or 129, Overtime Compensation for Nonexempt Employees, for details.

9.0 Safety and Worker's Compensation

Teleworkers must have work areas designed consistent with sound ergonomic principles and must use safe practices to avoid injury from improper use of equipment. Health and Safety representatives can provide information on design principles.

Worker's compensation liability for job-related injuries and illnesses and eligibility for accident disability benefits continues during the approved work schedule and in the employee's home work area as described in the Teleworking Agreement. Accidents must be reported to the Health and Safety Department.

AGCS shall have no liability whatsoever for any injuries to family members, visitors, and others in the employee's home. Employees should consult with their personal insurance carriers for advice.

Teleworkers are not to hold AGCS business meetings in their home office.

10.0 Disability Benefits

Employees on disability may not be required to work at home during the period of disability benefits. However, if an employee on disability asks to work at home, the manager should consult with the local health and safety representative and follow the medical professional's advice. If approved, the employee's status would change to active from disability.

11.0 Proprietary Information

The AGCS policy on business and scientific information as specified in HR policy 407 must be followed.

All AGCS proprietary information must be stored in a locked room, desk, or file cabinet when left unattended. Proprietary information must be disposed of by burning or shredding or must be returned to an AGCS facility for shredding.

12.0 Computers and Security

Protecting AGCS Depending upon the type of teleworker and the frequency of teleworking, employees may use either company-provided or their own computer equipment to perform their jobs from home. In either case, they must abide by the AGCS policies covering computer security.

12.1 Data protection: AGCS data is a valuable company asset. All teleworkers are responsible for protecting this data. Therefore, data files are to be kept on company network servers, and accessed via the appropriate remote access technology. If it is necessary to move data to a local computer for disconnected work, the teleworker is responsible to update the original at the first opportunity to get remotely connected. Teleworkers are also responsible for backing up their own systems so down time is minimized in the event of system failure. The only copy of company data should not reside exclusively on a remote device. Teleworkers are responsible for making any and all reasonable efforts to back up company data.

12.2 Virus protection: Computer viruses are a fact of life in the computer world. AGCS teleworkers are responsible for insuring that virus protection software from its is installed on their systems and enabled. Disabling or removing virus protection systems may result in loss of teleworking privileges. Teleworkers are also responsible for "safe" computing practices, such as avoiding downloads from unfamiliar sources and installing software only from disks provided by a manufacturer or its. its will maintain online information to assist in this effort and provide current information to the user community.

12.3 Use of company computer assets: AGCS may provide computer software or hardware for teleworkers' use. These assets are for business and not personal use. Software and hardware not licensed to or owned by AGCS may not be installed on AGCS owned computers without approval from its. If software is provided to an AGCS employee or contractor for use on a non-AGCS computer, that software must be removed and returned to its upon termination of employment or end of contract, or when the software is no longer needed for company use.

12.4 Software Piracy: It is AGCS policy to obtain proper licensing for all software in use on AGCS systems. AGCS employees and contractors are expected to comply with and support this policy. Therefore, all software installed on AGCS owned systems must be properly licensed. Users may not copy or distribute software without authorization from ITS and verification of proper license.

12.5 Use of other technology resources: AGCS provides a variety of technology resources, such as email systems and Internet access capability. AGCS users are to refrain from using these resources for non-business purposes.

13.0 Company-Provided Equipment and Support

Installation of non-AGCS approved software or hardware on AGCS owned equipment will result in loss of teleworking privileges. Company provided equipment is not to be used by non-AGCS employees (i.e., family members, friends, etc.).

13.1 Computer Hardware: AGCS will provide computer hardware assets for teleworkers' use based on the business need and the user's teleworking category (see Teleworker Category Matrix). Details on what can be provided and the necessary approval information can be found in the ITS Hardware Policy document.

13.2 Software: AGCS will provide computer software for teleworkers' use based on the business need and the user's teleworking category (see Teleworker Category Matrix, section 2 of the AGCS *Teleworking Handbook*). Software installation disks may be provided on a loan basis. The user is responsible for returning loaner disks by the time agreed to when the disks are checked out. Hardcopy documentation may not be provided, or may be available at additional cost billable to the user's department. Details on what can be provided and the necessary approval information can be found in the ITS Software Policy document.

13.3 Operating Systems: AGCS does not provide operating systems software for computer systems that are not owned by the company. A teleworker who will be using a personal system must provide a company approved desktop OS in order to receive support from the help desk. Currently approved and supported operating systems may be found in the ITS Operating System Policy document.

14.0 If Employee Owned Computer Systems Are Used:

➤ Any computer hardware expenses (to include maintenance, repairs, and insurance) are the employee's responsibility. Certain items such as modems may be provided at the discretion of ITS.

➤ Company data must be kept in separate directories or folders. It must be regularly backed up on removable computing media clearly marked as AGCS property (see section 12.1).

➤ Any software used for AGCS company business must be properly licensed. Only properly licensed software may be installed on a system used for an AGCS network.

➤ All AGCS information and AGCS network connections must be secured before leaving the work area. The employee is responsible for providing the same protection of company proprietary information at home as they do while working at the AGCS office.

15.0 Expenses

15.1 Reimbursable Expenses — Any reimbursable expenses must be authorized by the coach/ manager and charged to the employee's department or project. The Teleworking Agreement will specify expenses that the coach/manager may have authorized for reimbursement. For example, installation of a second telephone line and monthly fees may be approved by the manager as a reimbursable expense. To be reimbursed for other business expenses that may arise, the employee should seek management approval before incurring them. As needed, basic office supplies such as paper, pens, and clips will be provided by AGCS for the teleworker. Reasonable travel expenses may be authorized by the coach/manager for dedicated long distance teleworkers to return to the main offices of AGCS for meetings.

15.2 Non-reimbursable Expenses — Examples of non-reimbursable expenses are included in the following list. This list is not all inclusive; the coach/manager and the teleworking coordinator will confer and make any individual determination as required.

➤ Any costs related to remodeling and furnishing the home work space. The teleworker must insure that they have space that can provide a productive, safe work environment.

➤ Local commuting expenses between the work location and the regular AGCS work location.

➤ All household related expenses such as rent (or mortgage payments), heating, and electricity.

➤ Cost of insurance purchased purely for the teleworker's protection or benefit.

16.0 Termination of Teleworking Agreement

The Teleworking Agreement may be terminated at any time for any reason by the employee or manager. However, employees or managers wanting to terminate a teleworking agreement should discuss the request with one another at least 30 calendar days before terminating the arrangement. Notwithstanding the above, AGCS may modify or terminate a Teleworking Agreement and arrangement at any time for any reason. When the Teleworking Agreement is terminated, at management request, or when employment is terminated, all AGCS owned computer equipment, disks, and documentation must be returned to its, and all AGCS licensed software removed from non-AGCS owned systems.

17.0 Teleworking Handbook & Documents

The *Teleworking Handbook* contains guidelines, documents, and forms which are to be used with this policy. Signing the Teleworking Agreement does not affect the employee's employment status. The employee remains employed not by contract, but at will, meaning the employee and AGCS are each free to terminate the employment relationship at any time for any reason.

Appendix 3
TELECOMMUTER'S AGREEMENT

Sample Telecommuter's Agreement
California Department of Personnel Administration (www.dpa.ca.gov)

Both the manager and the telecommuter understand that home based telecommuting is a bilateral voluntary option and can be discontinued at either's request with no adverse repercussions.

The (agency) will pay for the following expenses:

➤ Charges for business related telephone calls

➤ Maintenance and repairs to state owned equipment

Claims will be submitted on a Travel Expense Claim along with receipt, bill, or other verification of the expense.

The (agency) will not pay for the following expenses:

➤ Maintenance or repairs of privately owned equipment

➤ Utility costs associated with the use of the computer or occupation of the home

➤ Equipment supplies (these should be requisitioned through the main office)

➤ Travel expenses (other than authorized transit subsidies) associated with commuting to the central office

Telecommute days are scheduled and will not be substituted without advance approval of the manager. In the office days will be _____ . Home office days will be _____.

Telecommuters must be available by phone during the core business hours of _____ to _____.

Use of sick leave, vacation, time off, or other leave credits must be approved in advance by the supervisor. Overtime to be worked must be approved in advance by the supervisor.

Telecommuting is not a substitute for dependent care and telecommuters must make regular dependent care arrangements.

The telecommuter has read and understands the agency's telecommuting policies and agrees to abide by those policies.

The telecommuter is to carry out the steps needed for good information security in the home office setting and has a copy of the agency's security requirements and procedures. The telecommuter agrees to check with her or his supervisor when security matters are an issue.

_____   _____

(Supervisor) (Date)   *(Telecommuter) (Date)*

Appendix 4
TELECOMMUTING AGREEMENT

US Office of Personnel Management
Sample Telecommuting Agreement

(Agencies may use or modify this sample agreement)

Between Agency and Employee Approved for Telecommuting on a Continuing Basis

The supervisor and the employee should each keep a copy of the agreement for reference.

Voluntary Participation

Employee voluntarily agrees to work at the agency approved alternative workplace indicated below and to follow all applicable policies and procedures. Employee recognizes that the telecommuting arrangement is not an employee entitlement but an additional method the agency may approve to accomplish work.

Trial Period

Employee and agency agree to try out the arrangement for at least (specify number) months unless unforeseeable difficulties require earlier cancellation.

Salary and Benefits

Agency agrees that a telecommuting arrangement is not a basis for changing the employee's salary or benefits.

Duty Station and Alternative Workplace

Agency and employee agree that the employee's official duty station is (indicate duty station for regular office) and that the employee's approved alternative workplace is: (specify street and number, city, and state).

Note: All pay, leave, and travel entitlement are based on the official duty station.

Official Duties

Unless otherwise instructed, employee agrees to perform official duties only at the regular office or agency-approved alternative workplace. Employee agrees not to conduct personal business while in official duty status at the alternative workplace, for example, caring for dependents or making home repairs.

Work Schedule and Tour of Duty

Agency and employee agree the employee's official tour of duty will be: (specify days, hours, and location, i.e., the regular office or the alternative workplace. For flexible work schedules, specify core hours and the limits within which flexible hours may be worked).

Time and Attendance

Agency agrees to make sure the telecommuting employee's timekeeper has a copy of the employee's work schedule. The supervisor agrees to certify biweekly the time and attendance for hours worked at the regular office and the alternative workplace. (Note: Agency may require employee to complete self-certification form.)

Leave

Employee agrees to follow established office procedures for requesting and obtaining approval of leave.

Overtime

Employee agrees to work overtime only when ordered and approved by the supervisor in advance and understands that overtime work without such approval is not compensated and may result in termination of the telecommuting privilege and/or other appropriate action.

Equipment/Supplies

Employee agrees to protect any government-owned equipment and to use the equipment only for official purposes. The agency agrees to install, service, and maintain any government-owned equipment issued to the telecommuting employee. The employee agrees to install, service, and maintain any personal equipment used. The agency agrees to provide the employee with all necessary office supplies and also reimburse the employee for business-related long distance telephone calls.

Security

If the government provides computer equipment for the alternative workplace, employee agrees to the following security provisions: (insert agency-specific language).

Liability

The employee understands that the government will not be liable for damages to an employee's personal or real property while the employee is working at the approved alternative workplace, except to the extent the government is held liable by the Federal Tort Claims Act or the Military Personnel (US) and Civilian Employees Claims Act (US).

Work Area

The employee agrees to provide a work area adequate for performance of official duties.

Worksite Inspection

The employee agrees to permit the government to inspect the alternative workplace during the employee's normal working hours to ensure proper maintenance of government-owned property and conformance with safety standards. (Agencies may require employees to complete a self-certification safety checklist.)

Alternative Workplace Costs

The employee understands that the government will not be responsible for any operating costs that are associated with the employee using his or her home as an alternative worksite, for example, home maintenance, insurance, or utilities. The employee understands he or she does not relinquish any entitlement to reimbursement for authorized expenses incurred while conducting business for the government, as provided for by statute and regulations.

Injury Compensation

Employee understands he or she is covered under the Federal Employee's Compensation Act if injured in the course of actually performing official duties at the regular office or the alternative duty station. The employee agrees to notify the supervisor immediately of any accident or injury that occurs at the alternative workplace and to complete any required forms. The supervisor agrees to investigate such a report immediately.

Work Assignments/Performance

Employee agrees to complete all assigned work according to procedures mutually agreed upon by the employee and the supervisor and according to guidelines and standards in the employee performance plan. The employee agrees to provide regular reports if required by the supervisor to help judge performance. The employee understands that a decline in performance may be grounds for canceling the alternative workplace arrangement.

Disclosure

Employee agrees to protect government/agency records from unauthorized disclosure or damage and will comply with requirements of the Privacy Act of 1974, 5 USC 552a.

Standards of Conduct

Employee agrees he or she is bound by agency standards of conduct while working at the alternative worksite.

Cancellation

Agency agrees to let the employee resume his or her regular schedule at the regular office after notice to the supervisor. Employee understands that the agency may cancel the telecommuting arrangement and instruct the employee to resume working at the regular office. The agency agrees to follow any applicable administrative or negotiated procedures.

Other Action

Nothing in this agreement precludes the agency from taking any appropriate disciplinary or adverse action against an employee who fails to comply with the provisions of this agreement.

Employee's Signature and Date: _____

Supervisor's Signature and Date: _____

(US Office of Personnel Management, www.opm.gov)

Appendix 5
TELECOMMUTING RESOURCES

Canadian Telework Association

www.ivc.ca

The Canadian Telework Association (CTA) is a Canadian nonprofit telework association dedicated to promoting telework in Canada. Members include individuals, corporate bodies (small, medium, and large), academics, and governments (at all levels). They come from dozens of countries.

Gil Gordon Associates

www.gilgordon.com

Operating since May 1995, this site consolidates a wide variety of information from around the world, and from many different perspectives, on the subjects of telecommuting, teleworking, the virtual office, and related topics. The site has been honored by several awards, including the Site Selection Insider's Web Pick of the Week award. Gil Gordon is an acknowledged expert in the implementation of telecommuting and telework.

JALA

www.jala.com

JALA is an international group of management consultants that was incorporated in California in 1982. Their activities are in four main areas:

- Telework, telecommuting, and virtual offices (JALA is a virtual firm)
- Applied futures research and forecasting
- Technology assessment
- Regional telecommunications planning

The website is designed to inform visitors and to demonstrate and enhance the services JALA provides to future and current clients. They've provided a number of resources to help visitors learn more about them, telework, and the future.

Telework.gov

www.telework.gov

The Office of Personnel Management (OPM) and the General Services Administration (GSA) have established this interagency website to provide easy access to information about telework in the Federal Government. The information contained on this website pertains only to Executive Branch agencies and employees.

Telework Recruiting.com

www.teleworkrecruiting.com

Telework Recruiting is dedicated to helping professionals in every field find telecommuting employment as quickly as possible.

The Telework Coalition

www.telcoa.org

Enabling virtual, mobile, and distributed work through education, technology, and legislation.

WorldatWork

www.workingfromanywhere.org

WorldatWork is a global human resources association focused on compensation, benefits, work-life and integrated total rewards to attract, motivate and retain a talented workforce. Founded in 1955, WorldatWork provides a network of more than 30,000 members and professionals in 75 countries with training, certification, research, conferences and community. It has offices in Washington, D.C. and Scottsdale, Arizona.

Appendix 6
MERRITT GROUP
TELECOMMUTE PROGRAM

Beginning September 11, 2009, Merritt Group will offer telecommuting as an agency-wide perk. We consider telecommuting to be a viable arrangement and one that supports the agency's commitment to work/life balance. The flexibility of telecommuting enables staff to eliminate stress from long commutes, and enjoy greater and more focused productivity. This program does not change the terms and conditions of employment with Merritt Group. The availability of telecommuting as a flexible work arrangement for employees of MGI can be discontinued at any time at the discretion of the company. To make this program work, there are a few policies that everyone must agree to:

Rules of the Road for Successful Telecommuting

The official Telecommute Day for the agency will be Friday. All employees are expected to work in the office Monday through Thursday. Of course, if you would prefer to work from the office on Fridays, that is perfectly acceptable too.

Clarity regarding your job and your accountabilities is fundamental: You and your manager need to be crystal clear about your responsibilities and expected results. The expectation is that you will perform the same job working from home, with the same duties and responsibilities, as if you were physically in the office (i.e., client deliverables, client calls, team priorities, media pitching). To be successful, you must know what your priorities are, what you need to accomplish and when, and develop a game plan for achieving results. If it's determined that productivity or performance is suffering because of this arrangement, some form of modification to the program might be necessary and will be evaluated on a case-by-case basis.

You should feel free to work during your peak energy times, but everyone must be working a full eight hour day just as if you were working in the office, including being available between the core hours of 10:00 a.m. and 4:00 p.m. or as needed by client or team meetings.

All team, group and corporate all-hand meetings will be scheduled Monday through Thursday to enable full staff participation and maintain open channels of communication.

The employee must be available upon reasonable notice to come to the office whenever the need arises for meetings, travel, training, etc.

Employees must have access to appropriate equipment needs (including phone, long distance plans, computer, and high-speed internet access). Equipment supplied by the employee will be maintained by the employee. MGI accepts no responsibility for the cost of or damage to employee-owned equipment.

Consistent with the agency's expectations of information security, employees will be expected to ensure the protection of proprietary company and client information accessible from their home office.

Telecommuting is not designed to be a replacement for appropriate child care. Although an individual employee's schedule may be modified to accommodate child care needs, the focus of the arrangement must remain on job performance and meeting business demands.

The employee will not engage in any non-agency activities while in official work status at the alternate work location. This includes such pursuits as family or personal business.

If personal matters arise while telecommuting, the employee will follow established leave/PTO policies at the alternate work station as though he/she were at the office.

Acknowledged and Agreed:

_____

Employee Signature   *Date*

Appendix 7
MERRITT GROUP CELL PHONE/ SMART PHONE POLICY

Updated September 1, 2009

Merritt Group appreciates the fact that most employees have personal cell phones and in many cases use them for company business and that most employees would prefer to use their own cell phone instead of having another cell phone issued by the company, and subsequently having to carry two phones. Therefore, the company does not purchase cell phones for employees nor will it pay for employees' cell phone plans directly. This allows you to invest in a phone that works best for you with the options you find most desirable.

The company also understands that smart phones are a valuable business tool and acknowledges the fact that smart phone technology with mobile email capabilities in many cases is instrumental to your effectiveness and efficiency in servicing our clients and performing your job. As a result, we have decided to offer up to a $500 reimbursement for the purchase of a smart phone to all employees. Smart phones must be able to receive emails remotely and sync up with our current Microsoft Office applications.

If you choose to purchase a phone, you must do an expense report and attach a copy of the invoice for the phone. Once the phone is purchased please contact Network Alliance to configure the device. This is a one-time reimbursement of up to $500. If the phone is lost, you will be responsible for replacing it with a device of equal functionality. In addition, Merritt Group will not be held responsible for repairs or maintenance required on your phone. We suggest getting an all-inclusive protection plan for your device.

In order to be reimbursed an employee must complete an expense report and provide a copy of their cell phone bill. Merritt Group will only reimburse up to the actual cell phone invoice amount. A copy of your monthly bill is required and must be submitted with an expense report within 30 days of the invoice date to be reimbursed.

Senior Staff	
VP and Above	$100 per month
Practice Directors	$ 80 per month
Account Supervisors	$ 80 per month
Account Managers	$ 80 per month
Junior Staff	
Senior Account Executives	$ 40 per month
Account Executives	$ 40 per month
Account Coordinators	$ 40 per month

Appendix 8
REMOTE ACCESS PERMISSION

In connection with your employment, XYZ Corporation "XYZ" is granting you permission to access certain of its systems ("Systems") remotely. This permission is subject to your strict adherence to the restrictions and limitations described below. The ability to access the Systems remotely is a privilege, not a right, which may be modified or revoked by XYZ at any time, without cause or notice.

1. Workplace Safety. You are responsible for regularly checking your remote workspace to ensure it complies with all health and safety requirements, including appropriate workstation configuration for reduction of repetitive stress and other similar injuries. XYZ does not control and has no responsibility or liability for ensuring the health and safety of the location from which you remotely access the Systems.

2. Use of Remote Access Technology. You must perform your work using only a computer provided by or specifically authorized by XYZ. All remote access must be made using only those procedures specified by XYZ and only for the purposes specifically authorized by XYZ. You are responsible for ensuring only XYZ authorized personnel (e.g., no family members or other non-employees) will have access to (i) XYZ provided computers, (ii) confidential and proprietary Information, or (iii) XYZ system access procedures. In the event you become aware of any unauthorized access to the Systems or XYZ' data or confidential information, you must immediately notify_____. You may not sell or otherwise dispose of any computer, laptop, or other equipment provided by XYZ. You must at all times ensure that access to the equipment is limited as described in this provision.

In particular, you may not leave unattended a computer remotely connected to the Systems (e.g., go to lunch with your home computer logged into our systems). You may not copy XYZ confidential or proprietary information to any form of Removable Media (defined below) without prior authorization from your supervisor or other authorized XYZ management. In the event XYZ confidential or proprietary information is reduced to printed form (e.g., by a printer or fax), all copies of such printouts must be returned to XYZ. Papers containing XYZ confidential or proprietary information that are no longer needed may not be disposed of at your remote work location. All such papers must be returned to XYZ for proper destruction. For purposes of this Agreement, "Removable Media" means portable or removable hard disks, floppy disks, USB memory drives, zip disks, optical disks, CDs, DVDs, digital film, memory cards (e.g., Secure Digital (SD), Memory Sticks (MS), CompactFlash (CF), SmartMedia (SM), MultiMediaCard (MMC), and xD-Picture Card (xD)), magnetic tape, and all other removable data storage media.

3.   Work Site Inspections. On reasonable notice, you agree to permit XYZ to inspect the location and computers from which you access the Systems remotely.

4.   Compliance with all Applicable Policies. Although you may be authorized to work at a remote work location, you will still be obligated to comply with all applicable XYZ employee policies and procedures, including those relating to information security, confidentiality, privacy, and use of information technology.

I understand that in signing this permission form I am acknowledging I have read, understand, and agree to be bound by the restrictions and limitations described above.

_____   _____

Employee Signature   *Date*   *Manager Signature*   *Date*